First published in 2012 by Zest Books
35 Stillman Street, Suite 121, San Francisco, CA 94107
www.zestbooks.net
Created and produced by Zest Books, San Francisco, CA

© 2012 by Zest Books LLC

Typeset in Sabon and Myriad Pro

Teen Nonfiction / History / Arts & Entertainment

Library of Congress Control Number: 2011942758

ISBN: 978-0-9827322-5-0

CREDITS
BOOK EDITORS: Dan Harmon and Karen Macklin
CREATIVE DIRECTOR: Hallie Warshaw
ART DIRECTOR/COVER DESIGN: Tanya Napier
GRAPHIC DESIGN: Tanya Napier
MANAGING EDITOR/ PRODUCTION EDITOR: Pam McElroy
RESEARCH EDITOR: Nikki Roddy
INTERN: Alice Dalrymple

TEEN ADVISORS: Amelia Alvarez, Ema Barnes, Anna Livia Chen, Huitzi Herrera-Sobal, and Felicity Massa

Manufactured in China
LEO 10 9 8 7 6 5 4 3 2 1
4500351786

Every effort has been made to ensure that the information presented is accurate. The publisher disclaims any liability for injuries, losses, untoward results, or any other damages that may result from the use of the information in this book.

THE END

50 APOCALYPTIC
VISIONS FROM POP CULTURE
THAT YOU SHOULD KNOW ABOUT

...before it's too late

LAURA BARCELLA

INTRODUCTION

I've always liked apocalypse-themed books and movies—especially zombie ones—and now, after putting in a zillion hours of writing and research on this book, I'm proud to consider myself a bit of an expert on this odd little mini-genre. One thing I'm sad to report is that there's an alarming lack of women in the coming apocalypse—at least as Hollywood imagines it. I found a few strong offerings by or about women, but I wished there were, well, more—especially since women have as much to lose in the end times as men do. Something else I learned? Considering the gloom and doom of the subject matter, some artists have managed to create surprisingly hilarious takes on the apocalypse (see the British "zomcom" *Shaun of the Dead*, page 122, and Stanley Kubric's now-classic film *Dr. Strangelove*, page 59). And perhaps the most useful bit of information I gleaned while writing this book (or not): If a human-sized plant that resembles asparagus begins to walk toward you, run.

As I immersed myself in writing *The End*, I realized just how many interesting ideas there are about the number of ways the world could end. It was overwhelming at first, having to narrow the list down to just fifty! People have been depicting the apocalypse through their art since, well, forever. And seeing these movies, listening to these songs, and reading these books was eye-opening, to say the least.

It was also a little scary! I found myself pondering "the end of days" way more than I ever had before. One night, a friend and I were driving home after a movie. It was after midnight on a Friday night and the usually bustling streets of our San Francisco neighborhood were surprisingly empty. Then we noticed—none of the stoplights or streetlights were working. The usually super-busy Mission Street was eerily dark and quiet. My first thought? Something like this: "We're done; it's finished; sayonara." Something terrible must have happened during those two hours we were in the movie theater and now … game over.

Fortunately, those fears passed quickly enough as we realized that certain apartments had lights on inside. Apparently the power had gone out; it was nothing more sinister than that. It made me realize, though, how deeply this apocalypse stuff had invaded my subconscious.

And that's probably the reason why the end of the world strikes such a nerve with artists. The idea of the apocalypse happening (and happening in our lifetime) is so major, so unthinkably big, that most of us can't handle dwelling on it—instead we just freak out, and spend the rest of the night watching reassuring sitcom reruns as an antidote. But the creators of these fifty works showed no fear; they tackled the apocalypse head-on, making it seem not only a little more imaginable, but a little less paralyzing. And some of them depict what might happen after an apocalypse—an idea that's both dour and hopeful.

No matter how you feel about the end of the world, I hope you enjoy reading this celebration of other people's ideas. There's something in here for everyone, and if you're a pop-culture junkie or an apocalypse buff, I don't think you'll be disappointed. And be sure to tell me what you think!

Laura Barcella
www.LauraBarcella.com

CONTENTS

12 Monkeys (1995)

DIRECTED BY Terry Gilliam
WRITTEN BY Chris Marker, David Webb Peoples, and Janet Peoples
COUNTRY OF ORIGIN USA

James Cole (Bruce Willis) prepares for his trip to the past in *12 Monkeys*.

A mind-bending sci-fi classic, *12 Monkeys* is set in a post-apocalyptic 2035, approximately forty years after most of the earth's population was destroyed by a mysterious virus. Because the surface of the Earth is now uninhabitable for humans, survivors live underground in cellars and tunnels. Researchers beneath Philadelphia have concluded that the virus was deliberately released by a terrorist group, the Army of the 12 Monkeys, and a scientist offers convicted prisoner James Cole (Bruce Willis) a reduced sentence if he goes back in time (time travel technology has been established) to collect a sample of the virus, with the hopes that a cure can be developed.

After mistakenly getting sent back to 1990 instead of 1996 as planned, Cole gets committed to a psychiatric hospital for his ramblings about time travel and the 12 Monkeys (in 1990 the virus hasn't broken out yet, so no one has a clue what Cole is talking about). In the hospital he meets crazy animal

More Movies Directed by Terry Gilliam
Monty Python and the Holy Grail (1975)
The Fisher King (1991)
The Imaginarium of Doctor Parnassus (2009)

👁 UNFORGETTABLE MOMENT

James Cole is haunted by a recurring nightmare in which he, as a child, watches as a man gets chased down, shot, and killed at the airport. At the end of the film, when Cole is trying to get through security to kill the bioterrorist (thereby preventing the spread of the virus), he gets shot dead. And Railly, who is with him, sees that a little boy (a younger Cole) is standing there, watching.

activist Jeffrey Goines (Brad Pitt) and a beautiful doctor named Kathryn Railly (Madeleine Stowe), who he starts to fall in love with. Cole begins to suspect that Goines—whose father is a noted virologist—has ties to the virus. Cole returns to the present time and then gets sent back again, this time to 1996. He finds Railly (who now believes Cole) and the two hunt down Goines. Goines, however, denies having any connection with the virus and even suggests that Cole may be tied to the impending apocalypse. Cole eventually gives up on his mission and decides to run away to Key West with Railly. At the airport, Railly spots the true culprit of the virus: an assistant at Goines's father's virology lab. She and Cole realize that the bioterrorist is about to get on a plane with the deadly disease. But in his attempt to kill the bioterrorist and save the world, Cole gets shot dead by security, and the terrorist goes on with his plan.

ⓡ EALITY FACTOR

The reason everyone dies in *12 Monkeys* is because of a virus believed to have been unleashed upon society by terrorists. Bioterrorism is the intentional release of biological agents like viruses, toxins, or bacteria into the world. There have only been a handful of successful bioterrorist attacks in the past twenty years, most of which have consisted of an agent spread via inhalation, and in the greater scheme of things, the damage from these attacks was fairly limited. But it does remain a viable threat, and the US has various practices in place to both prevent and defend ourselves against one, should it occur.

💡 The Inspiration

12 Monkeys was directly inspired by Chris Marker's 1962 French short film "La Jetee." Though Marker did not write *12 Monkeys*, he received a credit as one of the writers because of how much influence his movie had.

⚠ The Impact

✳ **Critics hailed *12 Monkeys*.** Reviewers said that the movie was a disturbing mental trip that stayed with you long after the film ended. Common Sense Media called it a "violent dystopian masterpiece" and *Time Out* magazine referred to it as "lunatic poetry."

✳ **It helped cement Brad Pitt's career.** Pitt was nominated for an Academy Award for Best Supporting Actor and won a Golden Globe for his role as Jeffrey Goines.

✳ ***12 Monkeys* offered a unique take on apocalyptic art.** Most apocalyptic movies offer a finite idea of what happens when the world ends. This movie leaves it up to viewers to decide what happens—and what doesn't. For instance, was Cole just crazy? Was it all a dream? Did it already happen? Or is it about to?

⚡ QUOTABLES ⚡

"You know what 'crazy' is? 'Crazy' is 'majority rules.'"
Goines says this to Cole, talking about how he's been mislabeled as crazy

*"Look at those assholes, they're asking for it.
Maybe people deserved to be wiped out."*
Cole to Goines as they watch a TV program at the psych hospital that featc featuring televised animal-testing

 **28 Days Later**
(2002)

DIRECTED BY Danny Boyle
WRITTEN BY Alex Garland
COUNTRY OF ORIGIN UK

In this realistically shot apocalyptic film, Jim (Cillian Murphy), a bike courier, wakes up from a coma in a deserted London hospital with no memory of how he got there or how long he'd been there. When he walks out onto the street, London looks like a ghost town: The streets are all empty and the cars have been left abandoned with their doors splayed open. After stumbling upon a rabid pack of humans in a church, Jim is saved by a quick-thinking duo, Selena (Naomie Harris) and Mark (Noah Huntley). They take him to their hideout and tell him what's happened: While Jim was in a coma, most of his fellow Brits (and possibly people throughout the world) had become infected by an ultra-contagious virus named Rage that is spread by infected laboratory primates. The virus, which is irreversible, causes people to twitch and spasm, uncontrollably vomit infected

Jim (Cillian Murphy) pits his craziest smile against a soldier's semiautomatic weapon in *28 Days Later.*

blood, and attempt to attack and kill as many people as possible.

The three band together to try and survive, but soon Mark gets infected and Selena kills him before he can infect anyone else. Now a duo, Selena and Jim soon find two more survivors, a man named Frank (Brendan

More Movies Directed by Danny Boyle

Trainspotting (1996)

Slumdog Millionaire (2008)

127 Hours (2010)

👁 UNFORGETTABLE MOMENT

As the sun goes down, Jim stumbles into a church and calls, "Hello?" After spotting huge piles of corpses scattered on the floor and in the pews, he catches the ominous glare of a few pairs of hollow zombiefied eyes staring back at him.

Gleeson) and his young daughter, Hannah (Megan Burns). The group hears a radio broadcast transmitted by soldiers who say they have "the answer to infection." The four head to the location, just outside Manchester, to find a fortified mansion under the command of Major Henry West (Christopher Eccleston). Before they get inside, Frank is infected, and a soldier kills him. Inside, it's all men, and West confesses to

Jim that he has essentially promised Selena and Hannah to his soldiers. Jim tries to rescue the women, but West orders his soldiers to execute Jim. Still, Jim manages to escape. He frees Selena and Hannah from the mansion after a bloody showdown with the soldiers, and the three of them drive out into the deserted world to try and find other survivors.

💡 The Inspiration

According to director Danny Boyle, writer Alex Garland was inspired to write *28 Days Later* after watching the opening sequence of *The Day of the Triffids* (page 50). In that scene, a man wakes up in a hospital to discover that a meteor shower has blinded everyone.

ℝEALITY FACTOR

The chance of there being a population-decimating virus has a relatively high reality factor among the various apocalyptic scenarios. Super-contagious, lethal viruses—like HIV, Ebola, and the bubonic plague—have already wreaked havoc on our population. That said, there's never before been a Rage-like virus that causes people to eat each other, and there's been no prediction by the medical community or otherwise that there will be one.

⚠ The Impact

⋇ **The film was a critical and commercial success.** Unlike many horror films, which fare well at the box office but less so with critics, *28 Days Later* garnered great reviews *and* made $82,719,885 worldwide.

⋇ **It's one of the few sci-fi/horror movies that actually feels and looks somewhat real.** This is partly because it was filmed in gritty digital video, has realistic dialogue, and its lead actor (Cillian Murphy as Jim) was then unknown (as opposed to being a recognizable Hollywood star).

⋇ **It led to a sequel, and a graphic novel.** The movie sequel, *28 Weeks Later*, came out in May 2007. It takes place six months after the Rage virus took over England. A graphic novel by Steve Niles, *28 Days Later: The Aftermath*, was published in April 2007 and focused on the time between *28 Days Later* and *28 Weeks*.

⚡ QUOTABLES ⚡

"If you look at the whole life of the planet, we ... you know, man, has only been around for a few blinks of an eye. So if the infection wipes us all out, that is a return to normality."

One of West's sergeants says this during Jim, Selena, and Hannah's first dinner at the creepy army barricade. The soldiers had been discussing whether it was possible for things to ever return to normal.

❋

"REPENT THE END IS EXTREMELY F--KING NIGH."

Graffiti on the wall of the church where Jim sees his first batch of infected people

99 Luftballons
(99 Red Balloons)

PERFORMED BY Nena (aka Gabriele Susanne Kerner)

WRITTEN BY Carlo Karges (German version, 1983) and Kevin Joseph McAlea (English version, 1984)

MUSIC BY Jörn-Uwe Fahrenkrog-Petersen (1983/4)

COUNTRY OF ORIGIN Germany and USA

Nena and her famous luftballons at a 2002 concert in western Germany.

" "99 Luftballons" is often thought of as a Cold War protest song.

It was originally performed in German by the band Nena, but was later rerecorded in English. The English version describes two people who stop into a toy shop to buy a bunch of red balloons one summer night, and then set them all into the air. Soon the military takes note that "something's out there" (they don't realize it's only balloons—they think it's some kind of UFO or military threat). This leads to a "red alert" as "panic bells" begin to sound. First the "war machine springs to life," then the "president is on the line," and soon the military has bombed everything to pieces and nothing is left but dust, the singer, and one red balloon.

More Songs by Nena
"Just Dream" (released in the USA in 1984)
"It's All In the Game" (1985)
"Carpe Diem" (2001)

👁 UNFORGETTABLE MOMENT

Toward the end of the English version of the song, Nena describes the unfolding war and cries out, "This is it, boys, this is war." She sings it in an almost giddy and gleeful way, as if to emphasize our culture's love of war.

The original German version is similar in theme, but a bit less specific than the English version. It also doesn't start in a toy shop.

℞EALITY FACTOR

There have been instances in which nuclear or military strikes have almost happened because of a perceived (but imaginary) threat. For instance, just past midnight on September 26, 1983, Russian Lieutenant Colonel Stanislav Petrov was in the commander's chair at the secret bunker where the Soviet Union reviewed its early warning satellites over the United States. Suddenly, Petrov received a flashing alarm that suggested that a nuclear missile had been launched from a US base. But Petrov had a gut feeling it was a false alarm (it was) and advised his colleagues of this. Thus, the Soviet Union didn't retaliate. The result could have been a full-scale nuclear war. So, though it's not likely, it is *possible* that a false alarm could occur again and devolve into full-scale nuclear war.

💡 The Inspiration

The English version was, of course, inspired by the German version. The songwriter/guitar player of Nena's band, Carlo Karges, has said that he was inspired to write this song when he saw balloons released into the air at a Rolling Stones concert in West Berlin. In light of the ongoing Cold War (also see the Inspiration section for *Endgame*, page 65), he wondered what would happen if the balloons crossed the Berlin Wall to the Russian side.

⚠ The Impact

✳ **"99 Luftballons" was a huge hit in America.** It reached #2 on the Billboard Hot 100 chart on two separate occasions. The song still holds up today and, despite its dark lyrical content, remains one of the most recognizable 1980s party songs.

✳ **The song was used as a fundraiser for Hurricane Katrina relief efforts.** The cable TV channel VH1 Classic played both the English and German versions of the "99 Luftballons" video over and over for one hour straight, from 2 to 3 pm EST, on March 26, 2006, as part of a $200,000 fundraising campaign for Mercy Corps' Hurricane Katrina relief efforts.

✳ **The ubiquitous song became a favorite cover song for other bands.** It was recorded by American pop-punk band Goldfinger (who sung it partially in German) in 2000, and by hardcore punk band 7 Seconds in 1986. *Harry Potter*–inspired "wizard rock" band Draco and the Malfoys also released a 2006 parody of the song that had the same tune but different lyrics (at the beginning of the song, for instance, they buy "chocolate frogs" from a magic shop instead of a "bag of balloons" from a toy shop).

⚡ QUOTABLES ⚡

"It's all over and I'm standing pretty in this dust that was a city / if I could find a souvenir, just to prove the world was here."

A lyric from the end of the song, in which the narrator describes standing alone with one red balloon in the post-apocalyptic rubble of her former city

✳

"Everyone's a superhero, everyone's a Captain Kirk"

The narrator describing the escalating war as the troops mobilize and jet fighters fill the sky

2012 (2009)

DIRECTED BY Roland Emmerich
WRITTEN BY Roland Emmerich and
Harald Kloser
COUNTRY OF ORIGIN USA

Kate Curtis (Amanda Peet) and her two kids are tired of *2012*. They look forward to better, less apocalyptic things in 2013.

On 2009, a geophysics team led by Dr. Adrian Helmsley (Chiwetel Ejiofor) learns that the Earth's core is heating up to dangerous levels due to a solar flare (an eruption of high-energy radiation on the sun's surface). Helmsley warns US President Thomas Wilson (Danny Glover) about the cataclysmic natural disasters that are bound to follow, but it isn't until 2010 that international leaders finally address the catastrophe and begin secretly building massive arks to ensure the survival of hundreds of thousands of people.

Three years later, in 2012, an easygoing sci-fi author named Jackson Curtis (John Cusack) has taken his kids camping in Yellowstone National Park. There he meets Charlie Frost (Woody Harrelson), a crazy conspiracy theorist who lives in a trailer and hosts a radio show devoted to the "end of days." Frost has a map with locations for the govern-ment's secret set of arks, and he tells Curtis about them, and about the Earth Crust Displacement—a theory that suggests major geological polar shifts can cause large-scale catastrophes. Frost believes the end is nigh and that the government is murdering officials who have tried to warn people about what's happening.

More Movies Directed by Roland Emmerich

Independence Day (1996)

Godzilla (1998)

The Day After Tomorrow (2004, page 47)

👁 UNFORGETTABLE MOMENT

Curtis's ex-wife and current boyfriend are shopping for supplies in the grocery store when a huge LA earthquake causes a massive rupture in the ground. The ground literally splits underneath their feet, opening up a gaping, cavernous hole and nearly killing them.

When Curtis and his kids get back to LA, they find massive earthquakes rattling the city, while millions of other people are dying in other disasters all across the world. Curtis, his ex-wife Kate (Amanda Peet), her boyfriend Gordon (Thomas McCarthy), and Curtis and Kate's kids rent a plane to escape LA. After flying back to Yellowstone, they use Frost's map to learn where the arks are—in China—and they head there.

ⓡ EALITY FACTOR

Over the last few decades, the Earth's core has been heating up—the average global temperature of the Earth has gone up at the fastest rate in recorded history, and the ten hottest years on record have all been after 1990. Scientists believe that this warming is from climate change sparked by our mistreatment and pollution of the planet. Though certain aspects of *2012* were based on reality, most people in the scientific community scoffed at the movie for being totally outrageous and unrealistic, and NASA even dubbed it "the most absurd and scientifically flawed sci-fi blockbuster in recent memory."

When they finally get to China, the group manages to stow away on the ark, and, in the end, the human race endures—at least, the humans lucky enough to have been on the arks.

💡 The Inspiration

2012 was partially inspired by Graham Hancock's *Fingerprints of the Gods*, a nonfiction book about the possibility of a technologically advanced civilization that was destroyed thousands of years ago, and which our contemporary world has for the most part failed to recognize. This ancient civilization was supposedly based in Antarctica; director Roland Emmerich has said that he first learned about the Earth Crust Displacement theory from Hancock's book.

⚠️ The Impact

✳️ **It drew huge crowds.** *2012* was #1 at the box office its first weekend, earning over $65 million. It did not, however, receive particularly good reviews.

✳️ **The movie drew attention—and criticism—for its promotional strategies.** Sony Pictures concocted an elaborate viral marketing campaign for the film, including building a website for the fictional Institute for Human Continuity. The site warned visitors that there was a 94 percent chance of "cataclysmic forces" destroying the Earth in 2012; it also pushed visitors to sign up for a lottery to, hopefully, be saved from peril.

✳️ **North Korea forbade its citizens from seeing *2012*.** North Korea's leader, Kim Jong-il, has stated that 2012 will be the year that North Korea will rise to prominence as a superpower. That notion is in direct conflict with the movie's central plotline that the world will end in 2012.

⚡ QUOTABLES ⚡

"You're telling me that the North Pole is now somewhere in Wisconsin?"
White House Chief of Staff Carl Anheuser, speaking to professor Frederic West about the Earth Crust Displacement theory

"Six months ago, I was made aware of a situation so devastating that, at first, I refused to believe it. However, through the concerted efforts of our brightest scientist we have confirmed its validity. The world, as we know it, will soon come to an end."
President Thomas Wilson delivering the news about the impending apocalypse to US citizens

🎭 play Angels in America: A Gay Fantasia on National Themes (1993)

WRITTEN BY Tony Kushner
COUNTRY OF ORIGIN USA

This seven-hour dramatic play is widely considered an apocalyptic work, though it's more about a societal apocalypse than a true end-of-times apocalypse. The play focuses on Prior Walker, a gay man dying of AIDS in the mid-'80s. As his health and personal life disintegrate he's visited by ghosts, as well as by an angel, who informs him that (surprise!) he's a prophet. As Walker gets sicker, his boyfriend, Louis, can't cope and leaves him. Walker's ex-boyfriend is a nurse named Belize who works for an unethical lawyer named Roy Cohn (who, besides being the only nonfictional character in the play, was also a closeted, homophobic lawyer in the 1980s who had unjustly prosecuted many innocent people for "communism" during the infamous McCarthy investigations). Cohn is gay and dying of AIDS, too, though he pretends to be straight and insists AIDS is for "homosexuals," and not world-shapers like him. (During this time period, it was scandalous to be gay, and people

Actors Ellen McLaughlin and Stephen Spinella making grand gestures in a Broadway performance of *Angels in America*, 1993.

with AIDS were discriminated against.) Other characters also become part of this crumbling landscape in which a terrible epidemic (AIDS) is killing people by the thousands.

More Plays Written by Tony Kushner

A Bright Room Called Day (1987)

The Intelligent Homosexual's Guide to Capitalism and Socialism With a Key to the Scriptures (2011)

👁 UNFORGETTABLE MOMENT

Walker lies in bed in his Manhattan apartment, sickened with disease and a broken heart. An angel crashes through his ceiling and explains that human progress upsets God and "shakes up heaven." The angel wants Walker to help stop this progress and restore the balance between heaven and earth.

In the Bible, plagues are often connected with the apocalypse, and many radical Christians at the time believed that the AIDS era was a sort of Judgment Day for gay people (they believed that being gay was a sin, and that AIDS was God's way of punishing gay sinners). In *Angels*, the plague is very real, but the main character is not seen as a sinner. He is the prophet of the play. He even goes blind and has revelatory visions about the end of the world. As evil forces like prejudice, greed, illness, and fear are conspiring to bring American society to an end, Walker is left with the task of trying to understand what it all means. Then, when Cohn dies, Belize steals his medicine (experimental drugs for AIDS that Cohn had gotten through his political connections) and gives it to Walker. This makes Walker healthy, so that he can continue to be a prophet for the gay community and the world.

🔍 REALITY FACTOR

By the mid-'80s, more than 38,000 cases of AIDS had been diagnosed in eighty-five countries, and the virus was affecting a disproportionate number of gay men. For those living in cities with a sizable gay population, the epidemic felt like an apocalyptic plague. That said, AIDS obviously did not bring the entire world to an end.

💡 The Inspiration

Tony Kushner is a gay playwright who lived through the '80s AIDS epidemic. He first wrote a poem called "Angels in America" after having a dream about an angel crashing through the ceiling of a friend who had AIDS (and who was also one of the first people Kushner knew with the virus).

The play's religious imagery was partially inspired by Kushner's curiosity about the Mormon faith. Supposedly, part of what sparked that curiosity was a six-month flirtation he'd had with a Mormon missionary in a Brooklyn subway. The city of New York was also an inspiration, as Kushner has said that New York has "a kind of real and unreal feeling" that conveys an apocalyptic vibe.

⚠ The Impact

✴ *Angels in America* made history. It became widely known as one of the most important plays of the twentieth century, and won both the Tony Award for Best Play (1993 and 1994) and the Pulitzer Prize for Drama (1993).

✴ The play gave birth to various adaptations. It became a 2003 HBO miniseries, starring Al Pacino, Meryl Streep, Emma Thompson, and Mary-Louise Parker, as well as an opera, which was first performed in Paris in 2004.

⚡ QUOTABLES ⚡

"Maybe I am a prophet. Not just me, all of us who are dying now. Maybe we've caught the virus of prophecy ... I believe I've seen the end of things. And having seen I'm going blind as prophets do, it makes a certain sense to me."
Walker speaking to Belize while at a friend's funeral

"This disease will be the end of many of us, but not nearly all, and the dead will be commemorated and will struggle on with the living, and we are not going away. We won't die secret deaths anymore. The world only spins forward. We will be citizens. The time has come."
Walker says this at the end of the play. He is talking about gay people, and how the time has come for them to be able to live openly.

TV ⚡ Battlestar Galactica

(1978–1979)

CREATED BY Glen A. Larson
COUNTRY OR ORIGIN USA

The original *Battlestar Galactica* sci-fi series only ran for one TV season, in 1978/79, but many fans consider it better than any of its various spin-offs and adaptations (see Impact section). The show is about an unnamed futuristic time during which humans are living on the twelve colonies of Kobol—a group of planets in a faraway star system. For the last thousand years, the humans on these planets have been at war with the Cylons, a species of human-designed, part-humanoid robots who turned on their makers. The Cylons finally propose peace, but then use the signing of the peace treaty as an opportunity to attack the humans' battlestars (huge aircraft-carrier-esque spaceships) and home planets. In this violent attack, they almost completely destroy the human race.

In this outer-space apocalyptic landscape, only one battlestar (named Galactica) survives, and it leads a fleet of ships that picks up and carries away the small number of

Three of the cast members from 1978's *Battlestar Galactica* decide to fight Cylons with what appear to be… flashlights?

More Shows Created by Glen A. Larson
Magnum, P.I. (1980–1988)
The Fall Guy (1981–1986)
Knight Rider (1982–1986)

Cylon-attack survivors. With nowhere else to go, Galactica's captain, Commander Adama (Lorne Greene), leads the humans—including Lieutenant Starbuck (Dirk Benedict), Captain Apollo (Richard Hatch), and Sergeant Boomer (Herbert Jefferson Jr.)—in pursuit of a mythical thirteenth colony, where they hope to live and restart society: a planet called Earth. They spend the entire series trying to get there, but alas, they never make it. In the course of their fruitless journey, the Galactica group also experiences more Cylon attacks, crash landings on other planets, food shortages, hijackings, and the discovery of an eerie new red planet.

💡 The Inspiration

For *Battlestar Galactica*, series creator Glen A. Larson linked up with John Dykstra, who had worked on the special effects for *Star Wars*. The duo allegedly used the writing of Erik Von Däniken (author of *Chariots of the Gods*) for inspiration for the series.

⚠️ The Impact

✳ **The one-year TV show started a neverending *Battlestar Galactica* craze.** There was a TV series called *Galactica 1980* as well as two movies: *Mission Galactica: The Cylon Attack* (1979) and *Conquest of the Earth* (1981). In December 2003, the Sci-Fi Channel broadcast a three-hour

Ⓡ EALITY FACTOR

Could humans living in another galaxy build a robot-type creature that could turn against them and annihilate our species? Theoretically it may be possible, but it's certainly not likely. For one, humans can't easily live on other planets because most planets (aside from Earth) don't have all the right conditions (water, sunlight, oxygen) for us to survive. And we have yet to build a creature that could avenge itself against us, but you never know what technology will bring. Some people do believe in technological singularity—the idea that the creation of a superhuman intelligence is possible, and potentially already underway.

reimagined miniseries named *Battlestar Galactica* that led to an online series in 2006 titled *Battlestar Galatica: The Resistance*. There have also been *Battlestar* comic books, novels, action figures, and video games. Yet another feature film is now in development.

✴ **It had a reputation for being a rip-off.** The movie *Star Wars* came out the year before the *Battlestar* TV show, and fans felt that the show had ripped off ideas and characters from the movie. Some of the purported rip-offs include *Galactica*'s version of Artoo Detoo: a robot dog named Muffit.

Critics also said *Battlestar* ripped off characters such as Han Solo (Starbuck), Luke Skywalker (Apollo), and Darth Vader (Baltar). That same year, 20th Century Fox Film Corporation sued Universal Studios (producers of *Battlestar Galactica*), claiming it had copied more than thirty distinct ideas from *Star Wars*. Universal responded that *Star Wars* itself was a copy of Universal's 1972 film *Silent Running*, directed by Douglas Trumbull, and countersued. Court proceedings lasted through 1982, years after *Battlestar Galatica* had gone off the air, and the suit ultimately ruled in favor of Universal Studios.

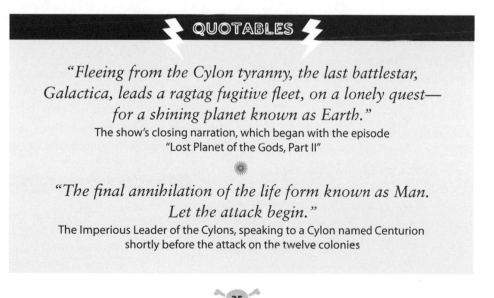

QUOTABLES

"Fleeing from the Cylon tyranny, the last battlestar, Galactica, leads a ragtag fugitive fleet, on a lonely quest—for a shining planet known as Earth."
The show's closing narration, which began with the episode "Lost Planet of the Gods, Part II"

"The final annihilation of the life form known as Man. Let the attack begin."
The Imperious Leader of the Cylons, speaking to a Cylon named Centurion shortly before the attack on the twelve colonies

The Big Swallow (2009)

CREATED BY Steve McGhee

COUNTRY OF ORIGIN Canada

Steve McGhee's *The Big Swallow* depicts a very bad day for fishermen.

On this vivid digital painting, Steve McGhee depicts a horrible storm occurring in Australia's idyllic Sydney Harbor. At the center of the piece (and the storm) is a massive whirlpool that is sucking two massive ships (and a whole bunch of small ones) down into its depths. On the periphery of this tragic, realistic-looking scene, everyday objects remain momentarily untouched: docked sailboats, houses, office buildings, and street lights. But there is a sense that all of it will soon be moving inward toward the giant whirlpool. In fact, the whole world may be on the verge of getting sucked down into the ocean.

This painting is not McGhee's only apocalyptic work, but it is his best known. His other apocalyptic images depict various major metropolitan hubs being destroyed in epic, spectacular fashion. McGhee shows tsunamis, tidal waves, airplane crashes, and

More Art by Steve McGhee

Water vs City (2008)

Ocean View (2009)

Earth Falls Away (2009)

fires in eerie, true-to-life detail. For instance, in *Water vs City*, New York City is being hit by a towering wall of water and cars in the street are being tossed up into the wave. In *Breathing Underwater*, floodwaters creep up the stairs of a deserted London's Bank Street subway station; in the background, a dark twister is perched, about to come around the corner. These disasters seem unreal in their grandiosity—they are kind of like the movie *2012* (page 17) come to life—but some of them have a chilling resemblance to real-life events like 9/11 and Japan's massive March 2011 earthquake and tsunami.

ℝEALITY FACTOR

There are, of course, whirlpools in nature. Because of rising and falling tides. In the ocean whirlpools are currents that move in a rotating direction and sometimes have a downward pull, known as a vortex. Whirlpools have been known to take lives—in 1913, two boys were killed when they were sucked into a whirlpool at Niagara Falls, and in 2011, a man was killed at a Bahamas resort when he was trapped underwater by the extreme force of the whirlpool suction outlet in a hotel hot tub—but the majority of whirlpools aren't large or powerful enough to cause mass deaths like the one in McGhee's painting. And they're certainly not strong enough to bring about the end of the world.

💡 The Inspiration

McGhee says his work is inspired by disaster movies and the unpredictable world that we live in. His work aims to comment on how little control we really have as humans (even though we try so hard to control and manipulate our environment). For *The Big Swallow*, McGhee was also inspired by water. He loves to swim, but acknowledges the inherent danger in the ocean.

⚠ The Impact

* McGhee's apocalyptic work has gotten recognized as fine art. Despite its gruesome nature, McGhee's work has been hailed as technically exceptional digital art. In 2009, *The Big Swallow* won the General Photoshop category in the National Association of Photoshop Professionals (NAPP) Fourth Annual Photoshop Awards, and in 2010, his piece *Last Flight Home* won in the Best Digital Art category of the Annual Design Awards competition.

✳ **McGhee's work shows hope in the face of a disastrous event.** After Japan's deadly March 2011 earthquake and tsunami, McGhee was asked to contribute a piece for a relief effort campaign organized by an artist collective called To Japan with Love. McGhee's work, *Earth Hardens*, depicts a pink lotus blossom floating on a tranquil, sunlit lake, showing that serenity and peace can arise even after there's been great destruction.

⚡ QUOTABLES ⚡

"Inspiration comes from the epicenter of the horrific and the heavenly in equal measure. Sometimes it shoots through my brain like a bullet, other times it floats down to me on angel's wings. Either way ... it gives me a place to put feelings that would otherwise be too overwhelming and it is the only way to be truly original, truly groundbreaking."
Steve McGhee, describing his work on Inspiredology.com, 2011

"I have always been fascinated by things which arrogant man has no control over — natural disasters, deadly disease, sharks growing legs, stuff like that."
Steve McGhee describing his work in an email interview, 2011

Blindness
(1995)

WRITTEN BY José Saramago
COUNTRY OF ORIGIN Portugal

In José Saramago's *Blindness*, an unnamed city becomes afflicted with white blindness, a condition where the afflicted can see nothing but white. A young man is the book's first victim—he is suddenly struck blind while driving down a city street—but the disease soon spreads to all of the people he's had contact with, including the eye doctor who attempted to diagnose the young man's odd symptoms. Reacting to the panic, the government decides to quarantine all of the victims in an old asylum and split them into three wards. The eye doctor's wife fakes being afflicted with the condition in order to stay with her husband.

Armed guards shout orders from a distance and throw food in the yard for the prisoners, and things quickly descend into pandemonium. Anyone who tries to escape is shot dead. The doctor's wife, however, remains

The eye doctor's wife (played by Julianne Moore in the movie adaptation) leads a group of the blind down a very menacing hallway in *Blindness*.

immune to the disease, and, as the only person with sight intact, begins to feed, clean, organize, and lead her new blind "family." Soon, under the influence of a nasty tyrannical leader, the people in Ward 3 gain control of the food rations and start to demand jewelry and sex in exchange for food. The doctor's wife kills the vicious leader of Ward 3, provoking a war among the prisoners, and

More Books Written by José Saramago

The Gospel According to Jesus Christ (1991)
The Tale of the Unknown Island (1998)

In the book's opening scene, drivers are waiting at a stoplight when a man fails to move his car after the light turns green. Cars behind him sound their horns, and people begin knocking on his window to see what's wrong. He is stricken with a frantic desperation and mouths at them: "I am blind." This is the first victim of white blindness.

one woman sets fire to the asylum. Then, the doctor's wife leads her blind group to freedom outside, but society has completely broken down. There is no running water, dead bodies and excrement fill the streets, and blind wanderers fight one another for food and resources. The doctor's wife and her new blind family must try to survive in this horrid, apocalyptic landscape, and they are just starting to rebuild their lives when suddenly and inexplicably, the blind begin regaining their sight.

Ⓡ EALITY FACTOR

In real life, there are no forms of blindness that are contagious between humans. The term "white blindness" is linked to a virus called myxomatosis, which afflicts rabbits and causes swellings, conjunctivitis, blindness, and death. But this is not the same condition that Saramago describes in his novel. So it's not very likely that a blindness epidemic will cause an apocalyptic outcome any time soon.

💡 The Inspiration

In a speech he gave when he won the Nobel Prize in Literature in 1998 (see Impact), Saramago suggested that *Blindness* was inspired by the way he feels society is becoming blind to injustice. He mentioned the loss of respect humans have for one another, and how the powerful feed off the weak.

⚠ The Impact

✳ **The book has become a classic in its own time.** José Saramago received the Nobel Prize in literature for the book in 1998 and wrote a follow-up called *Seeing*, which takes place in the same unnamed country and features some of the same characters.

✳ **The book was turned into a major Hollywood film.** *Blindness*, directed by Fernando Meirelles and starring Julianne Moore, premiered in 2008 and was selected as the opening film at that year's Cannes Film Festival, one of the oldest and most prestigious film fests in the world.

✳ *Blindness* **angered the National Federation of the Blind.** In 2008, the organization protested the movie version because in it "blind people ... are portrayed as incompetent, filthy, vicious, and depraved ... unable to do even the simplest things like dressing, bathing, and finding the bathroom."

QUOTABLES

"If we cannot live entirely like human beings, at least let us do everything in our power not to live entirely like animals."
The doctor's wife says this to those at the asylum, encouraging them not to behave like cretins just because the world around them is falling apart

"Why did we become blind? I don't know. Perhaps one day we'll find out. Do you want me to tell you what I think? Yes, I do. I don't think we did go blind; I think we are blind, blind but seeing; blind people who can see, but do not see."
Part of an exchange between the doctor and his blind patients at the end of the novel, after they finally begin to regain their sight. (Saramago doesn't use proper grammar in much of the book as a way of inviting the reader to fumble through the sentences the way the characters fumble around in the dark.)

book A Canticle for Leibowitz (1960)

WRITTEN BY Walter M. Miller Jr.

COUNTRY OF ORIGIN USA

Canticle for Leibowitz is an apocalyptic classic that still ranks high on many sci-fi hit lists. Its intricate story spans thousands of years and is told in three sections. The first part, "Fiat Homo" (Let There Be Man), is set in a new dark ages, six hundred years after a nuclear war (known as the Flame Deluge) had destroyed most of civilization in the early 1960s. The world is now overtaken by beasts and criminals. Anyone with knowledge of the old world (doctors, scientists, teachers, etc.) is scorned and even killed in the Simplification—a huge backlash against intellect and knowledge. The church has become one of the only places left where knowledge is collected and celebrated.

The rare intellectuals of this society often speak of an iconic hero named Isaac Edward Leibowitz—a "booklegger" from after the nuclear war who had risked his life to smuggle books to safety. At some point he was caught and killed, and a monastery

THE CLASSIC BESTSELLER AND A LANDMARK OF 20TH-CENTURY LITERATURE

A CANTICLE FOR LEIBOWITZ

WALTER M. MILLER JR.

Author of *Saint Leibowitz and the Wild Horse Woman*

The past can't help repeating itself in *A Canticle for Leibowitz*.

More Books Written By Walter M. Miller Jr.

Saint Leibowitz and the Wild Horse Woman (novel, finished by Terry Bisson; 1997)

"Death of a Spaceman" (short story, 1954)

"Six and Ten Are Johnny" (short story, 1952)

🔍 UNFORGETTABLE MOMENT

In the first part of the book, Brother Francis Gerard is on a vigil in the desert when he comes across a wanderer. The wanderer helps him find a rock to use to build a shelter, but as he picks up the rock, Brother Francis notices that beneath it is an entrance to an ancient fallout shelter, where he finds a stash of old handwritten notes and cryptic texts on old memo pads. These notes seem to have been written by Leibowitz, his order's original founder.

called the Albertian Order of Leibowitz in the Southwestern US desert is now trying to make him a saint. We eventually learn that Leibowitz was a Jewish physicist (and later a priest) who saved not just books but grocery lists, lottery tickets, and drawings with the intention of passing them down to future generations.

The second part of the book, "Fiat Lux" (Let There Be Light), takes the reader to another future time period in which science and technology are booming again, and electricity has been reinvented. This new era is embodied in the confident scientist Thon Taddeo; meanwhile Dom Paolo, a monk, doubts these new technological inventions and tries to maintain the sanctity of his faith.

In the book's last section, "Fiat Voluntas Tua" (Thy Will Be Done), the world is again drifting toward a nuclear war. The Order of Leibowitz has lost most of its power, but it readies a spaceship to send a group of clergy and children into space to escape the impending nuclear catastrophe and build a new life on another planet.

🔍 REALITY FACTOR

A Canticle for Leibowitz, at its heart, is a story about how history repeats itself when people fail to learn from it. And if you look at the rise and fall of civilizations, or the thousands of years of war in human history, it's easy to see that the causes for the apocalypse in *A Canticle for Leibowitz* are fairly realistic.

💡 The Inspiration

Author Walter M. Miller Jr. enlisted in the US Army Air Forces shortly after the bombing at Pearl Harbor, and he spent much of World War II in Italy and the Balkans as a radioman and tail gunner on B-25 bombers. On one of these Italian missions, he participated in the destruction of one of the oldest monasteries in the Western world—Italy's Benedictine monastery, the Abbey of Montecassino. On February 15, 1944, the monastery was destroyed by American bombers. The attack was based on a fear that the abbey was being used as a lookout for the German defenders, but a later investigation proved that it was a refugee shelter and that the only people who had been killed in the bombing were innocent civilians. The whole thing was a traumatic experience for Miller, and in 1947 he converted to Catholicism in part because of this experience.

⚠ The Impact

✳ *A Canticle for Leibowitz* **is considered a sci-fi classic.** It has never been out of print since it was first published, and received the Hugo Award (a prestigious science fiction prize) in 1961 as the best novel.

✳ **The book lived on in other formats.** A fifteen-part radio serial was adapted and broadcast on NPR in 1981, and in 1993, BBC Radio broadcasted a dramatization of the first two books, "Fiat Homo" and "Fiat Lux."

⚡ QUOTABLES ⚡

"Because if a man is ignorant of the fact that something is wrong, and acts in ignorance, he incurs no guilt, provided natural reason was not enough to show him that it was wrong. But while ignorance may excuse the man, it does not excuse the act, which is wrong in itself."

The abbot of the St. Leibowitz monastery, talking to a doctor about the "mercy camps" (crematoria set up to dispose of radiation victims)

Cat's Cradle (1963)

WRITTEN BY Kurt Vonnegut
COUNTRY OF ORIGIN USA

Kurt Vonnegut, author of *Cat's Cradle*, is not amused.

Cat's Cradle is a black comedy, an epic tragedy, and a scathing send-up of science and religion as practiced in mid-century America. The story begins with the book's narrator "John" seeking out the children of Felix Hoenikker, a scientist who'd helped develop the atomic bomb. John wants to write a book about what famous people were doing when the US dropped the bomb on Hiroshima. Instead, he gets drawn into the Hoenikker family and learns that Felix had worked on another horrifying invention which (apparently) never made it off the drawing board: a kind of ice known as ice-nine.

Regular ice melts at 0 degrees Celsius (C; 32 degrees Fahrenheit), but ice-nine remains solid up to 45.8 degrees C (114 degrees Fahrenheit, and instantaneously aligns all water molecules into its own solid structure. If you dropped a single molecule of ice-nine into the Atlantic, all the world's water would freeze, and in a chain reaction, the ice-nine would seep into rivers, streams, and oceans. If it rained, that water would freeze upon contact with ice-nine, too. Weather would go haywire, plants and animals would die of thirst, and any living thing that touched the ice-nine would immediately have its own water molecules frozen and solidified. Yikes!

More Books Written by Kurt Vonnegut
Welcome to the Monkey House (1968)
Slaughterhouse-Five (1969)
Breakfast of Champions (1973)

👁 UNFORGETTABLE MOMENT

Bokonon produces many psalms, rhymes, and new words as the leader of Bokononism. His final writing, which he shares with John on the frozen mountain at the end of the story, is this: "If I were a younger man, I would write a history of human stupidity; and I would climb to the top of Mount McCabe and lie down on my back with my history for a pillow; and I would take from the ground some of the blue-white poison that makes statues of men; and I would make a statue of myself, lying on my back, grinning horribly, and thumbing my nose at You Know Who."

Both John and the Hoenikker children end up traveling to a small Carribbean island ruled by an ailing dictator ("Papa" Monzano) and his foil (a trickster guru named Bokonon, who has founded a cynical state religion). John falls in love with Papa's daughter, Mona, but learns that she is engaged to Franklin Hoenikker, a son of Felix's who's been missing for many years and is slated to take over for Papa upon Papa's imminent death.

ℝ EALITY FACTOR

In the book, ice-nine is supposed to create unusually stable ice crystals at a temperature of 44 Celsius (109 Fahrenheit). It would look just like normal freezing. It sounds cool (actually it sounds freezing), but so far no one has developed a world-ending form of water… as far as we know!

With Papa on his deathbed, Franklin suddenly offers the dictatorship and Mona to John, who accepts. But then, just after the two announce the change of plans to Papa, he puts a gift from Franklin to his tongue: ice-nine! Franklin's secret weapon instantly turns Papa into an ice-corpse, and when a plane crashes into the cliffs above Papa's castle, it causes a landslide which brings half the castle—and Papa's body with it—into the ocean. All the world's water turns to ice-nine within seconds. The world is essentially over at this point, but it takes a few more months of wandering and mass suicide before John and Bokonon, seemingly the last men on Earth, meet up on the island's mountain and exchange last words before dying.

💡 The Inspiration

Having survived the fire-bombing of Dresden (a city in Germany) during World War II, author Kurt Vonnegut knew what horrors could be unleashed when science, technology, and politics got together and ran amok. The very idea of ice-nine, together with *Cat's Cradle*'s references to the atom bomb, played into common mid-century fears that science had developed weapons that it could no longer control.

⚠ The Impact

✳ **It has been taught to generations of high school students.** The *New York Times* noted in Vonnegut's 2007 obituary that even though *Cat's Cradle* only sold about five hundred copies initially, it became widely read in high school English classes.

✳ **It's been a gateway for many young readers.** Because it's taught so widely, *Cat's Cradle* has been the beginning of many a young reader's journey into Vonnegut's larger body of work. It's also considered a gateway to postmodern literature, since once a young reader is hooked on Vonnegut, she's likely to stumble on to other postmodern authors like Thomas Pynchon, Vladimir Nabokov, and William S. Burroughs.

⚡ QUOTABLES ⚡

"Tiger got to hunt, bird got to fly; Man got to sit and wonder 'why, why, why?' Tiger got to sleep, bird got to land; Man got to tell himself he understand."
One of Bokonon's religious writings

✳

"'Maturity,' Bokonon tells us, 'is a bitter disappointment for which no remedy exists, unless laughter can be said to remedy anything.'"
John reflecting on the pessimism inherent in trickster guru Bokonon's religion. (Bokononism tends to focus on the uselessness of existence.)

Children of Men (2006)

DIRECTED BY Alfonso Cuarón

WRITTEN BY Alfonso Cuarón, Timothy J. Sexton, David Arata, Mark Fergus, and Hawk Ostby

COUNTRY OF ORIGIN UK

Julian (Julianne Moore) and Theo (Clive Owen) conspire with a bunch of overenthusiastic skiers in *Children of Men*.

This modern apocalyptic flick is set in London in the year 2027. All of the women have mysteriously lost the ability to bear children, and as a result the planet is comprised wholly of people age eighteen and up. What this means: Humans are poised to become extinct in the not-too-distant future. Meanwhile, most of the world's governments have collapsed into chaos. England still has some sense of civil society, but that's also made it a prime destination for illegal immigrants. In response, the city has turned into a police state, with armed officers routinely and brutally rounding up and detaining people.

Then it's discovered that an illegal immigrant named Kee (Claire-Hope Ashitey) is miraculously eight months pregnant. Fearful that Kee might fall into the wrong hands, immigrant activist Julian (Julianne Moore) calls upon her estranged husband, Theo (Clive Owen), and asks for help. Julian hopes to take Kee to the Human Project, an organization of infertility-research scientists based on

More Movies Directed by Alfonso Cuarón

Great Expectations (1998)

Y Tu Mamá También (2001)

Harry Potter and the Prisoner of Azkaban (2004)

At the start of the movie, clusters of somber, scared-looking Brits squeeze into a storefront to catch the news, blaring from an overhead TV screen. Eighteen-year-old Baby Diego—the youngest person left on the planet—has been stabbed to death in a bar brawl. The onlookers' horrified reaction to the news is less about the dead young man and more about what his death represents: Any hope for the future is gone.

Portugal's Azore islands, in the middle of the Atlantic Ocean. Theo reluctantly agrees, but Julian is killed (shot, in an incredible action sequence) soon afterward, and the group gets in trouble with the police. Even so, Theo, Kee, and Miriam (a midwife) continue their journey, and Kee does finally make it to the Human Project's boat (appropriately named *Tomorrow*), which will take her to its headquarters. Sadly, Theo is shot, and dies as this is happening.

REALITY FACTOR

We never find out what caused the mass infertility in the movie. In real life, there are a multitude of factors that make it hard for a woman to conceive, and, according to the Centers for Disease Control and Prevention, nearly 12 percent of women of childbearing age today struggle with fertility problems. But, the chances of all the women, all over the world, becoming infertile at the same time? Slim to none.

💡 The Inspiration

The movie was inspired by and loosely based on the 1992 book *The Children of Men* by English author P.D. James. The book was also about a society in which no more children were being conceived. The film, however, had a lot of plot differences from the book.

The title of both book and film were inspired by the Bible. The phrase "children of men" comes from verse three of Psalm 90: "Thou turnest man to destruction; and sayest, Return, ye children of men." Most believe that the first part means that mankind will be wiped out by God because of humans' grave propensity to sin. The second part ("and sayest, Return, ye children of men") is interpreted different ways. Some believe that the "return" is simply man's return to dust; others believe the "return" here signifies that Christ will call those who repent to resurrection after the destruction. Either way, it can be seen as an end-of-times, apocalyptic reference.

⚠️ The Impact

✳️ **The movie was a commercial and critical smash.** On September 22, 2006, the film debuted at #1 in the UK, earning £1.28 million (about $2 million US) during its opening weekend. As of now, the film has earned $35,552,383 in the US. The film was also nominated for three Oscars: Best Adapted Screenplay, Best Cinematography, and Best Film Editing.

✳️ **The movie offered a haunting vision of what a world without children would look like.** Though the movie's chase scenes and shoot-outs are intense to begin with, the film's violence is even more visually arresting due to the flat grey landscapes it's set in. The lack of youth, laughter, and sunlight echo the lack of hope in the population as a whole.

⚡ QUOTABLES ⚡

"Infertility is God's! punishment."
The words on a sign held by a religious protester

✳️

"As the sound of the playgrounds faded, the despair set in. Very odd, what happens in a world without children's voices."
Miriam's observation as she, Theo, and Kee hide from police inside a school

The Colony

(2009–present)

DIRECTED BY Nick Murray
COUNTRY OF ORIGIN USA

The Colony is a reality show on the Discovery Channel that takes ten people of various ages, races, and backgrounds and places them in a different apocalyptic landscape each season. The fictitious scenario—which is the supposed result of a global catastrophe or a viral outbreak that has killed off most of the human race, means that the participants (or "colonists") are isolated for the equivalent of ten episodes, and tested to see how they handle life without basics such as electricity, running water, fuel, security, communications, or a functioning government.

The colonists—who so far have included a nurse, a martial arts instructor, a carpenter, an aerospace engineer, and an auto mechanic—are forced to build a workable society, and handle extreme physical and emotional stress in places like an abandoned warehouse outside of Los Angeles, or ten abandoned acres on the Gulf Coast of Louisiana (an area that was previously destroyed by Hurricane Katrina). They have to find their own food, endure solitude and massive sleep deprivation, and face concocted dangers like aggressive gangs and other hostile outsiders (played by actors) who threaten to steal their resources. The colonists learn to be resourceful, scavenging for supplies, purifying water, and constructing survival implements like a solar cooker, a shower system, and a greenhouse. Experts in relevant fields like engineering, psychology, medicine, and disaster preparedness are commentators on the show, and make sure that the colonists don't actually die in the process.

The Inspiration

Discovery Channel is known for gritty reality shows like *Deadliest Catch, American Loggers,* and *Man vs. Wild.* Though there is no documented inspiration for this show, it was probably inspired in part by society's insatiable craving for worst-case, end-of-the-world entertainment, along with the

More TV Shows Produced by John Gray
Deadliest Catch (2005)
30 Days (2008)
The Virus (2010)

👁 UNFORGETTABLE MOMENT

In the second episode of season two, the gang wanted to use a tractor to build an alternator (to make electricity). In a modern world, there'd be a diesel pump where the gang could fuel up the tractor—but not in this apocalyptic landscape. So the group decided to try making their own biofuel with animal fat from a huge stash of rotting pig carcasses they'd recently discovered in a truck. They stripped down to their skivvies and took the decomposing pigs out of the truck, retching and gagging, and flung the dead pigs onto the ground. Extra bonus: many close-up shots of squirming maggots.

more recent cultural trend of creating a reality show out of anything and everything. It may have also been more directly influenced by another 2005 Australian reality show called *The Colony*, in which modern families were sent to Australia to see how they would cope if they were forced to live in New South Wales two hundred years ago, when it was a penal colony.

ⓡ EALITY FACTOR

Despite being a reality show, *The Colony* isn't necessarily an accurate portrait of what a post-disaster area would look like. The whole scenario is constructed, and the producers hire experts to step in and rescue the colonists from any real danger. It does a good job, though, of showing the multiple skills that would be required to survive in this sort of environment.

⚠ The Impact

✳ *The Colony* **was the first apocalyptic reality show.** Sure, it's an odd premise, but the "What would you do if disaster hit?" aspect has drawn curious viewers to the show—especially those who think we may be headed for a similar disaster state in the US sometime soon. (Living in poverty with no clean water and electricity is, of course, already a reality for lots of people in developing or war-torn countries.)

✳ **Season two helped bring money to a Katrina-ravaged disaster zone.** The town of Chalmette, Louisiana (part of the greater New Orleans area), was decimated by Hurricane Katrina in 2005. By filming the show in that town, and hiring local residents to help with the production, the show brought an estimated $5 million to the community.

✳ **It was praised as being thought provoking.** Both viewers and critics liked the show's emphasis on the practical aspects of survival, and found it to be less fluffy than some other reality shows in which people just complain, fight, and make senseless drama.

⚡ QUOTABLES ⚡

"Being a country boy, there's a lot of things I remember—like making gas from animal fat."
Louisiana native Robert, who suggested that they try producing biofuel from dead pigs

✳

"We shouldn't be using our filtered water ... It's just not right, because our drinking water is far more precious than hair looking nice."
New York–born Sian's response to Becka from Colorado, who had decided to wash her hair with an unidentified bottle of something "bubbly"

art The Course of Empire: Destruction of Empire (1995)

CREATED BY Sandow Birk

COUNTRY OF ORIGIN USA

This painting is the fourth in a series titled "The Rise and Fall of Los Angeles." The five oil-on-canvas images depict the same spot: a section of land in the Hollywood Hills of Los Angeles. In the first painting, there are dinosaurs and cavemen roaming; the second painting shows cowboys, orange groves, and taco stands symbolizing Spanish colonialism and Spanish influences in general; the third painting is a vision of the contemporary city; and in this fourth painting we see an apocalyptic destruction of the city in a near future time. The final painting in the series is set in a distant, post-apocalyptic future. Though the sky is blue and plant life endures, there are no humans around and the landscape looks neglected.

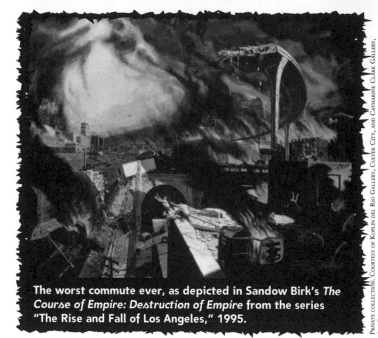

The worst commute ever, as depicted in Sandow Birk's *The Course of Empire: Destruction of Empire* from the series "The Rise and Fall of Los Angeles," 1995.

Destruction of Empire is probably the scariest of the five images. Huge waves of black smoke billow up from a raging fire that has consumed apartment buildings and some overturned vehicles (the result of an apparently collapsed highway overpass). A

More Art by Sandow Birk

"In Smog and Thunder: The Great War of the Californias" (series, 2000)

"The Depravities of War" (series, 2007)

Sniper's View of the White House (2010)

massive bridge is also in mid-collapse, and a big red truck is about to career off the edge. The Hollywood sign is hazily visible through tufts of gray smoke. There are a few people depicted in the painting—a man and a woman are attempting to climb over a partition or a wall of some kind—but the way the man is reaching out for the woman in front of him, it's hard to tell whether he's trying to help her or hurt her. There are also a couple of people on the ground. One appears to be sitting—either dazed or hurt—and the other is flattened beneath an object that must have crushed him. Of course, the biggest unanswered question that arises when looking at this painting is "What happened to cause all this destruction?" And although the painting doesn't directly tell us, the artist has said that he imagines the cause to be "a combination of earthquake and fire" triggering catastrophic results.

REALITY FACTOR

For Californians, the threat of another big earthquake is always present. (Because California sits on a major fault line, it's not a matter of if, it's a matter of when). So Birk's vision of a massive earthquake rattling Los Angeles is realistic. According to a 2008 report, California has more than a 99 percent chance of being hit with a magnitude 6.7 or larger earthquake in the next thirty years. The 1906 earthquake in the San Francisco Bay Area caused hundreds of deaths and injuries, and also led to extensive fires and citywide damage. And more recently, the Loma Prieta quake in 1989 collapsed several important roads and freeways and left a lot of the city in ruins. That said, it's a bit of a stretch to imagine that one earthquake would cause a total worldwide extinction of modern society, which is what the final painting in the series seems to imply.

💡 The Inspiration

Birk's "Rise and Fall of Los Angeles" series is based on nineteenth-century American artist Thomas Cole's series "The Course of Empire," which depicts the rise and fall of ancient Rome between 150 CE and 476 CE. In Birk's series, Rome is replaced by Los Angeles, which the artist believes can, in a twisted way, be seen as the apex of modern civilization, on account of its modernity and celebrity appeal (as well as its overcrowdedness and terrible pollution).

⚠ The Impact

✳ **This painting inspired introspection in California residents.** It reminded Angelenos (people who live in Los Angeles) that, despite all of the distractions and glamour of their big-city lives, it could all fall apart at any time.

✳ **This series was an essential part of Birk's quest to become a successful, well-known artist (later).** The paintings in this series were some of Birk's earliest works, and they helped get his name out to the public. He went on to become super-respected in the art world and has since shown work at the Metropolitan Museum of Art in New York, the de Young Museum in San Francisco, and Biblioteca Nazionale Centrale di Roma in Rome.

⚡ QUOTABLES ⚡

"As an Angeleno and as a surfer, I never wanted to have to move to New York to be an artist, and so a constant under-theme of my works has been the city itself, trying to make Los Angeles be the most important city in the world."
Birk, explaining his passion for Los Angeles

✳

"My idea was to take the Romantic view of human civilization that Cole had and twist it."
Birk, describing the series

movie The Day After Tomorrow (2004)

DIRECTED BY Roland Emmerich

WRITTEN BY Roland Emmerich and Jeffrey Nachmanoff

COUNTRY OF ORIGIN USA

The Statue of Liberty goes wading out to sea in *The Day After Tomorrow.*

Jack Hall (Dennis Quaid) is a paleoclimatologist who believes that melting polar ice—a result of global warming—is disrupting the North Atlantic current and that within weeks or even days, a new Ice Age will be upon us, causing the death of most life on Earth. Hall attempts to warn the vice president, but his ideas are laughed off as exaggerations. Soon, though, dramatic disasters begin to take place all over the world: a snowstorm in New Delhi, a hailstorm in Tokyo, and a series of devastating tornadoes in Los Angeles.

Hall's teenage son, Sam (Jake Gyllenhaal), is visiting New York City to participate in an academic competition with a few classmates (including his crush, Laura, played by Emmy Rossum). While there, a massive "superstorm" hits, with winds and rains causing Manhattan's congested streets to flood. The storm intensifies and a huge tidal wave hits Manhattan, causing more flooding and killing thousands. Sam and his friends hole up with hundreds of others in the New York Public Library. While there, Sam calls his father, who advises him to

More Movies Directed by Roland Emmerich

Independence Day (1996)

2012 (page 17; 2009)

👁 UNFORGETTABLE MOMENT

Soon after they stumble up the steps of the New York Public Library, Sam's crush, Laura, heads back out to the street, to fetch something a foreign woman had accidentally left behind. As Laura bends into the cab to retrieve the woman's purse, Sam notices a tidal wave looming a block or two behind her. As the deadly wave sweeps around the corner and annihilates everything—buses, taxis, people—in its path, Sam wades into the water to try to save Laura from the oncoming destruction.

wait out the storm inside, since going outside could cause people to freeze instantly.

Meanwhile, the president of the United States orders everyone in the southern states to evacuate, sending a deluge of refugees crossing illegally into Mexico. Jack and two friends set out to track down Sam in NYC as the superstorm worsens. After astronauts confirm the storm's dissipation, Jack and friend Jason (the other survivor) finally arrive in New York. The library is covered

® EALITY FACTOR

In *The Day After Tomorrow*, global warming causes a sudden climate change, creating a "superstorm" that triggers massive weather disasters across the world. Could this ever happen in real life? Though the movie is based on *some* valid scientific principles, no, a sudden global warming-induced climate shift could not cause the kind of instant weather chaos that appears in the movie.

in snow, but fortunately Jack finds Sam's group alive. As the main characters are evacuated, they can see during their flight over the city that lots of other people have also made it through the storm. At the movie's end, the astronauts look down at Earth from the Space Station. Most of the northern hemisphere is covered in ice and snow, and there is a big decline in pollution.

💡 The Inspiration

The Day After Tomorrow was inspired by the book *The Coming Global Superstorm*. It was written by Art Bell, former host of the paranormal talk radio show "Coast to Coast AM," and Whitley Strieber, author of nonfiction book *Communion: A True Story* (Strieber's bestselling account of being abducted by aliens).

⚠ The Impact

✳ **In 2008, Yahoo! Movies listed *The Day After Tomorrow* as one of the Top 10 Scientifically Inaccurate Movies.** One of Yahoo! Movies' main gripes? That most of Antarctica would have to melt in order to submerge New York City as much as it was in the movie.

✳ **The film garnered mixed reviews from both the science community and laypeople.** Global warming skeptic Patrick J. Michaels dubbed the film "propaganda," and Joseph Richard Gutheinz Jr., a college instructor and retired NASA office of inspector general, called the movie "a cheap thrill ride." Still, the movie was #2 at the box office (behind *Shrek 2*) on the Memorial Day weekend it was released.

⚡ QUOTABLES ⚡

"How am I supposed to adjust, Sam? Everything I've ever cared about, everything I've worked for … has all been preparation for a future that no longer exists."
Laura, talking to Sam about her perfectionistic academic tendencies and how, in the face of the apocalypse, none of it was worth it

✳

"Mankind survived the last Ice Age. We're certainly capable of surviving this one. All depends on whether or not we're able to learn from our mistakes."
Jack, discussing the current catastrophe with friend Jason as they trek toward NYC to rescue Sam

✳

"This tornado just erased the Hollywood sign. The Hollywood sign is gone. It's just shredded."
A reporter describing how the Hollywood sign was destroyed by a tornado in Los Angeles

The Day of the Triffids (1981)

DIRECTED BY Ken Hannam

WRITTEN BY Douglas Livingstone and John Wyndham (book author)

COUNTRY OF ORIGIN UK

The Day of the Triffids begins with Bill Masen (John Duttine) waking up in a London hospital with his eyes obscured by bandages. He narrates his thoughts into a handheld recorder, and as he does so we learn about his job working with a species of poisonous plant that walks on three legs and attacks humans with a long stinger. Because Masen had been around these "triffids" since childhood, he (unlike most people) is resistant to their sting, which is why he managed to survive the earlier venom attack that damaged his eyes.

Put off by the eerie quiet that surrounds him in the hospital, Masen decides to go ahead and remove his bandages. When he looks around he quickly realizes that the hospital is almost empty. Masen heads out onto the London streets only to find freaked out, zombie-like people staggering around in search of food and help. Everyone appears

Actress Janette Scott hones her hide-and-seek skills in the 1962 film version of *The Day of the Triffids.*

More Directed by Ken Hannam
Dangerfield (TV series, 1997–1998)
The Bill (TV series, 2000–2001)

👁 UNFORGETTABLE MOMENT

Masen and Josella are driving in a car when they pull to a stop on a London street. A growing herd of blind people hear the car and realize a sighted person must be behind the wheel. Desperate for food and help, the zombie-like masses descend on the car, pounding on the windows, trying to open its doors, and shouting for the passengers to come out.

to have been blinded (somehow) by a strange green meteor shower that occurred the night before. He spots a young, sighted woman named Josella (Emma Relph) being forced at knifepoint to act as a guide for an old blind man, and after he steps in on her behalf, they fall in love.

Meanwhile, with 95 percent of the population now blind, society has begun to break down. Masen and Josella—now desperate for hope after finding her family dead—make their way to the University of London, where a band of polygamous sighted people are trying to rebuild society. Not everyone around the university is so kind-hearted though, and before long Masen is separated from Josella, kidnapped, and forced to serve as the guide for a dangerous group of blind people led by a man named Coker. Fortunately, a disease kills these people off and Masen is able to reunite with Josella and settle on a farm with a few other people. Unfortunately, the farm is surrounded by triffids, so they have to fight constantly to keep out the evil plants before moving to the Isle of Wight, where someone has cleared the triffids, making it an easier place to settle. (Phew.)

💡 The Inspiration

The BBC miniseries was based on a 1951 book of the same name by sci-fi author John Wyndham. He decided to start writing sci-fi soon after leaving the army in 1946, and was inspired by H.G. Wells's novel *The War of the Worlds* and Jules Verne's *Journey to the Centre of the Earth*.

🔍 REALITY FACTOR

The notion of everyone going blind by looking at a meteor shower is good stuff for a sci-fi production, but it's definitely not based on reality. Sure, we've all heard our moms' warnings about going blind by looking directly at the sun, but have no fear—it's just a myth. It is theoretically possible that one could go blind that way, but it's highly unlikely. Still, you can hurt your eyes from looking at the sun, so it's best to avoid it.

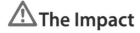

⚠ The Impact

✴ *The Day of the Triffids* got a shout-out in the famous cult classic *The Rocky Horror Picture Show.* The killer plants are mentioned in a song called "Science Fiction," which includes the line "I really got hot when I saw Janette Scott fight a triffid that spits poison and kills." Janette Scott played the role of Karen Goodwin in the 1962 film version; Goodwin is a character that isn't in the 1981 miniseries.

✴ **The miniseries influenced the apocalyptic film *28 Days Later.*** Alex Garland, who wrote the screenplay for *28 Days Later* (see page 11), has said that he was inspired to write his film after watching the opening scene of *The Day of the Triffids.* The main character in *28 Days Later* also wakes up in a hospital to notice that, while he was sleeping, the world outside was ending.

 QUOTABLES

"I've been doing a lot of thinking … I've had enough. I'm chucking the job. I'm fed up with triffids. I want to be loved. I want to breed puppies and plant potatoes."

Masen, speaking into his handheld tape recorder at the beginning of the first episode

"Most women want babies. A husband is just a logical means to an end."

Josella to Masen, soon after they meet the leader of the burgeoning polygamous sect, who had just announced that every woman in the group would have to procreate (probably with more than one man) and bear children. It's unclear if she's joking or serious.

Deep Impact

(1998)

DIRECTED BY Mimi Leder

WRITTEN BY Bruce Joel Rubin and Michael Tolkin

COUNTRY OF ORIGIN USA

No disaster movie is complete without a traffic jam, and *Deep Impact* is nothing if not a disaster movie.

When teen astrologer Leo Biederman (Elijah Wood) spots something strange in the sky he quickly alerts a professional astronomer—who discovers that the object is a massive comet on a collision course with the Earth. Unfortunately, the astronomer dies in a car accident on his way to spread the news about the comet, and it's only a year later that TV news reporter Jenny Lerner (Tea Leoni) stumbles onto suspicious government information about a woman named Ellie. After poking around, Lerner realizes that Ellie is actually E.L.E., an acronym for Extinction-Level Event. When US President Tom Beck (Morgan Freeman) finds out that Lerner knows about the comet, he goes on TV to tell the world that the deadly comet is expected to hit within months.

The US has been working secretly with Russia to build a spacecraft, the Messiah, from which astronauts will shoot down the comet with nuclear missiles. But the missiles only break the comet into two pieces. The small piece is poised to land in the Atlantic Ocean with an impact that has the potential to send a 350-foot tidal wave inland, annihilating New York City.

More Directed by Mimi Leder

L.A. Law (TV series, 1987)

ER (TV series, 1994–2009)

Pay It Forward (movie, 2000)

On the day the asteroid is projected to hit, TV reporter Lerner and her estranged father are standing together on a beach near the vacation house they frequented in Lerner's youth. Despite their painful history, they recognize the magnitude of the impending disaster and realize it's their last chance to forgive one another. They stand hugging on the beach when the first comet hits far out in the Atlantic Ocean. As a frighteningly tall wall of water begins to rush toward the pair, Lerner hides her face on her father's shoulder.

The larger piece will hit Canada, causing even more damage. As a backup, the government has constructed a huge underground cave that will hold one million Americans. Beck, Biederman, and Lerner are preselected for admission along with the world's top scientists, teachers, soldiers, and artists; most everyone else is selected through a national lottery. Those selected head into the cave; others who live at the coast try to flee inland to higher ground by car (which only leads to the world's worst gridlock).

Ⓡ EALITY FACTOR

Earth has been hit by a number of comets and asteroids over the years. In fact, according to *Scientific American* magazine, we can expect about one large asteroid to impact Earth every hundred million years or so (some scientists believe this is what killed the dinosaurs), so the general premise of *Deep Impact* is scientifically sound. That said, the likelihood of it happening in our lifetime is pretty small.

The first comet hits and the tidal wave takes out New York. The crew on the Messiah (which is still in space) makes a last-ditch attempt to blow up the second comet, and although they don't survive, the mission succeeds, and humanity is saved from total extinction.

💡 The Inspiration

Director Mimi Leder has said she was inspired by the way that people react in the face of major disasters. She wanted to encourage viewers to think about how they might feel and what they might do if they found out the world was about to end. *Deep Impact*'s producer, Richard Zanuck, has also said that *Deep Impact* was inspired by the 1951 film *When Worlds Collide* (see page 146), in which a star is on a deadly collision course with Earth.

⚠ The Impact

⁕ *Deep Impact* **had a deep impact on viewers.** People appreciated the thought-provoking storyline. And even though the flick was competing that summer with the Hollywood-star-studded *Armageddon* (a similar disaster flick that came out just two months later), *Deep Impact* opened with higher numbers and got stronger reviews than its competitor.

⁕ **Mimi Leder became known as a leading female director in male-driven Hollywood.** *Deep Impact* set a record for the biggest opening weekend for a woman-directed film, grossing over $41 million. Catherine Hardwicke stole this honor with *Twilight* in 2008, which took in an opening-weekend total of about $70 million.

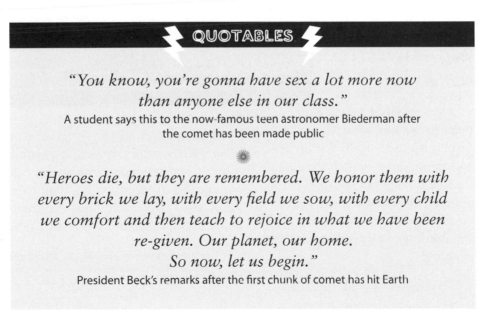

QUOTABLES

"You know, you're gonna have sex a lot more now than anyone else in our class."
A student says this to the now-famous teen astronomer Biederman after the comet has been made public

"Heroes die, but they are remembered. We honor them with every brick we lay, with every field we sow, with every child we comfort and then teach to rejoice in what we have been re-given. Our planet, our home.
So now, let us begin."
President Beck's remarks after the first chunk of comet has hit Earth

play Dog Act

(2004)

WRITTEN BY Liz Duffy Adams
COUNTRY OF ORIGIN USA

"Shakespeare meets *Mad Max*" is the way the play's co-director Jennifer Kraus described this madcap, post-apocalyptic romp. The play follows the journey of actress Rozetta "Zetta" Stone (get it?) and her friend Dog (a former human man who has chosen to undertake "voluntary species demotion" as atonement for an unknown crime). Zetta is a vaudeville performer traveling by foot to put on a show for the king of China, and although the rest of her troop has been eaten by cannibals, Zetta is determined that the show must go on—especially since China is known in legend as a land of peace and riches.

It's a long and dangerous walk to China through a New England landscape that's been annihilated by an unnamed catastrophe, and which also has sudden and vio-

Jo-Jo (Becky Byers) and Vera (Liz Douglas) just milling around in Flux Theatre Ensemble's production of *Dog Act*.

lent seasonal changes. The landscape isn't completely empty though; it's peopled with the aforementioned cannibalistic Scavengers, and ruled by violent tribes with names like the Nuevo Aztecs, Radical-Agrarian-Utopians, and the Skinhead-Skateboarders Union.

More Plays Written by Liz Duffy Adams
Neon Mirage (2006)
Or (2009)

👁 UNFORGETTABLE MOMENT

The play includes five musical numbers, meant to be performed using the kind of instruments that would be available in an end-times wasteland: guitars made from crutches, broken plates for percussion, and so on. As the keepers of the last embers of humanity's artistic flame, vaudevillians preserve and carry cultural artifacts from before the fall. Unfortunately, these have been passed from mouth to ear so many times that songs and expressions are now as mangled as they would be at the end of a game of telephone. A rousing performance of "Swing Low, Sweet Chariot" includes choruses like "sng yo, street Harriet," and "sling Joe, fleet cherry-Anne."

Zetta and Dog happen upon another wandering pair of vaudevillians, Vera Similitude (get it?) and her companion, Jojo. Vera specializes in "truths" (nothing but the truth, if not the *whole* truth) and Jojo is a wild, spastic storyteller. The four band together, but it's not easy: Vera is all sweetness and civility on the outside, but cold and calculating underneath, and Jojo is a loose cannon. To make matters worse, although none of the others know about it, Jojo has two bloodthirsty Scavengers trailing after her.

® REALITY FACTOR

The play never reveals what kind of catastrophe led to the ruined landscape and total social collapse. Depending on your view of society, the play's vision of a world of murderous nomads may be very realistic!

It all comes to a head when the four rehearse the play for the Chinese king. Some stagefighting turns tragic (the old stabbed-with-a-real-knife-not-a-stage-knife trick), and then the murderous pair of Scavengers crash into the scene. Vaudevillians are held sacred by the Scavengers' queen, but will these two honor the taboo against spilling actors' blood?

💡 The Inspiration

In an interview with thehappiestmedium.com, the playwright explained why she chose a post-apocalyptic world for *Dog Act*. She said she didn't feel the story could exist in the present because she liked the "heightened theatrical language" of her invented future dialects. She devised different forms of speech for all the different tribes.

⚠ The Impact

✴ **The play won a prestigious award for its first performance.** *Dog Act* was awarded San Francisco's 2004 Will Glickman Playwrights Award for best new play in the Bay Area, putting Adams in the company of playwrights like Denis Johnson and Tony Kushner.

✴ **It puts an entertaining new spin on a familiar genre.** Although the play seems like a theatrical version of *The Road* (see page 113; with more singing and slapstick), it owes more to the bleak world and tragicomic tramps of Samuel Beckett's play *Waiting for Godot*. Adams adds warmth, quirky musical numbers, and zany wordplay to the classic *Godot* formula familiar to most theatergoers.

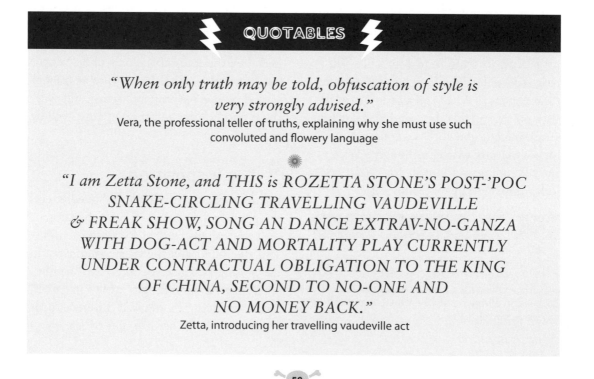

⚡ QUOTABLES ⚡

"When only truth may be told, obfuscation of style is very strongly advised."

Vera, the professional teller of truths, explaining why she must use such convoluted and flowery language

✳

"I am Zetta Stone, and THIS is ROZETTA STONE'S POST-'POC SNAKE-CIRCLING TRAVELLING VAUDEVILLE & FREAK SHOW, SONG AN DANCE EXTRAV-NO-GANZA WITH DOG-ACT AND MORTALITY PLAY CURRENTLY UNDER CONTRACTUAL OBLIGATION TO THE KING OF CHINA, SECOND TO NO-ONE AND NO MONEY BACK."

Zetta, introducing her travelling vaudeville act

![movie] Dr. Strangelove or: How I Learned to Stop Worrying and Love the Bomb (1964)

DIRECTED BY Stanley Kubrick

WRITTEN BY Stanley Kubrick, Terry Southern, and Peter George (pen name: Peter Bryant)

COUNTRY OF ORIGIN England

Dr. Strangelove (Peter Sellers) suffers from a very strange sort of tic in Stanley Kubrick's famous black comedy.

In this satire on nuclear war, the clearly deranged US Air Force Brigadier General Jack D. Ripper (Sterling Hayden) decides the United States must attack the Soviet Union with nuclear bombs right away to stop the Soviet's alleged communist conspiracy to contaminate US citizens with water fluoridization. Ripper seals off Burpelson Air Force Base and sends his bomber wing off to attack the Soviet Union. Upon hearing this news, US President Merkin J. Muffley (Peter Sellers), who had no say in the matter, organizes a panicked last-minute meeting with his advisors, including General "Buck" Turgidson (George C. Scott) and Dr. Strangelove (also Peter Sellers), a weird wheelchair-bound German scientist with a mechanical arm who uses the term *führer* when addressing the president. Muffley then calls Soviet premier

More Movies Directed by Stanley Kubrick
Lolita (1962)
The Shining (1980)
Full Metal Jacket (1987)

👁 UNFORGETTABLE MOMENT

When the Soviet ambassador, Alexei de Sadeski (Peter Bull), tells the US president and his advisors about the perilous Doomsday Machine, the United States suggests that the Soviets de-trigger it. de Sadeski explains that de-triggering it will *also* trigger it. Though the situation is obviously grave, Dr. Strangelove seems to delight in what he sees as a brilliant device that has no exit strategy.

Dmitri Kissof (who was found drunk at a Moscow brothel), and the two devise a plan to shoot down the American planes.

But there is a problem: The Soviets have a "doomsday machine," which is a defense system that, if triggered, will eliminate all life on Earth and engulf the world in nuclear fallout for ninety three years. The doomsday machine is set to explode automatically if a bomb gets dropped on the Soviet Union. Terrified of the potential apocalypse, American leaders try to figure out the recall code to bring the bomber planes back and cancel

their missions. In the end, all the planes are brought back, except one (it doesn't have a working radio). That plane goes on to release a nuclear bomb, making the doomsday machine's activation inevitable. The film ends with the image of nuclear bombs exploding all over the world, accompanied by the Vera Lynn song "We'll Meet Again."

💡 The Inspiration

Dr. Strangelove or: How I Learned to Stop Worrying and Love the Bomb is an adaptation of author Peter George's acclaimed 1958 Cold War thriller *Red Alert*, which focuses on the threat of nuclear war and its power to extinguish the face of humanity. *Red Alert* is not a comedy, though. The movie was also inspired more generally by the hostile global politics of the Cold War (see Impact section, next page; also see Inspiration for *Endgame*, page 66, for more about the Cold War).

ℝ EALITY FACTOR

It's hard to believe that a nuclear war could happen based on an accident or misunderstanding, but there have been close calls in the past (see Reality Factor in "99 Luftballoons," page 14). As long as there are nukes, an accident will always remain a small possibility.

⚠ The Impact

✳ *Dr. Strangelove* **has become a classic.** It is ranked the thirty-fourth greatest film of all time on the Internet Movie Database, and was also nominated for four Academy Awards (it didn't win any, though) and seven BAFTA (British Academy of Film and Television Arts) Awards (it won four).

✳ **It controversially satirized the possibility of nuclear war.** At the time, the Cold War was going strong and the country had been brought to the brink of nuclear war in 1962 by the Cuban missile crisis, so nuclear war seemed like a viable threat to Americans. Kubrick made the film to show how ridiculous war was, and to poke fun at the seemingly unintelligent people placed in charge of nuclear weapons. It was not common for movies back then to question, criticize, or poke fun at national or military leaders, so the movie was seen as controversial—but audiences really loved it.

⚡ QUOTABLES ⚡

"There were those of us who fought against it, but in the end we could not keep up with the expense involved in the arms race, the space race, and the peace race. At the same time our people grumbled for more nylons and washing machines. Our doomsday scheme cost us just a small fraction of what we had been spending on defense in a single year."
Soviet Ambassador de Sadeski, explaining why his country created the Doomsday Machine

✸

"I will not go down in history as the greatest mass-murderer since Adolf Hitler."
President Muffley, discussing what will occur if Ripper's nuclear attack on the Soviet Union isn't stopped

 **Earth Abides** (1949)

WRITTEN BY George R. Stewart

COUNTRY OF ORIGIN USA

Earth Abides is considered a landmark (and underappreciated) science-fiction work. It depicts the decimation of modern society after a hugely destructive plague called the Great Disaster wipes out most of civilization. Set near Berkeley, California, in the 1940s, the book centers on a graduate student named Ish (short for Isherwood) Williams. A loner type, Ish is busy doing solitary ecology research in a mountain cabin when the virus strikes. When he finally leaves his cabin, he finds out that most of the population is dead. Eventually Ish stumbles upon some survivors, and he manages to find a wife, Em (despite the incredibly slim pickings). They have kids in an attempt to form a fledgling community (a "tribe") that will hopefully lay a foundation for a future civilization. Ish longs to preserve culture and history as he remembers it, but most of his peers don't care about his stories from the past.

Only one of Ish and Em's children, Joey, embraces lofty pursuits like reading, geography, and geometry. Because of this, Joey

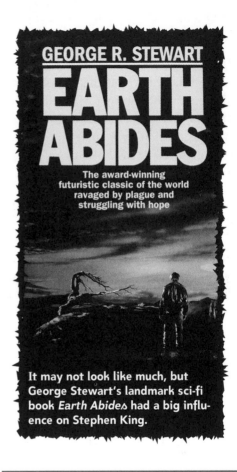

It may not look like much, but George Stewart's landmark sci-fi book *Earth Abides* had a big influence on Stephen King.

More Books Written by George R. Stewart

Storm (novel, 1941)

Fire (novel, 1948)

is Ish's favorite son, as well as his hope for the future. When Joey dies in a typhoid outbreak, Ish is devastated by the loss, but soon realizes that, in this society, it's more important for people to know how to filter water than to philosophize, so he focuses on teaching the community practical survival skills instead of academics. He teaches them to plant corn and make bows and arrows. Soon his lessons start to sink in, and he can see his efforts making an impact. The years roll by, and the tribe eventually merges with another one. Finally, in his old age, Ish becomes "the last American" (the last person born before the Great Disaster)—an almost godlike figure to the younger people in the now-expanded tribe.

🔍 REALITY FACTOR

The cause of the near-extinction of human life in *Earth Abides* is a super-contagious measles-like virus which causes a pandemic. The likelihood of a global pandemic (like 2009's bout of swine flu) happening again is high, especially with the availability of rapid worldwide transit today. But it won't be the measles. We have a vaccine for that nowadays. Of course, it could be something similar to the measles, since vaccines usually only work for the exact disease for which they were created.

💡 The Inspiration

The main character in *Earth Abides*, Ish, was inspired by Ishi, the last surviving Native American of the Yahi tribe (he died in 1916). His tribe was killed off by starvation and a series of violent massacres.

⚠ The Impact

✴ *Earth Abides* **is one of American litera-ture's earliest attempts at post-apocalyptic science fiction.** It provoked many future authors and filmmakers to meditate on what it might look like if most of human-kind died off.

✴ **The book was boundary-breaking in its portrayal of interracial marriage.** Em is black and Ish is white, but Stewart paints them as steady equals in their partnership and in their burgeoning tribe. This may not seem like a big deal now, but it was a bold move on the author's part, because interracial romance was still scorned (and interratial marriage was actually illegal in some states) at the time of the book's publication.

✴ **It had an impact on famous sci-fi/hor-ror scribe Stephen King.** In his nonfiction book *Danse Macabre*, King wrote that his post-apocalyptic novel *The Stand* (page 125) was inspired by *Earth Abides*.

⚡ QUOTABLES ⚡

"Crisis acute."
The headline on a newspaper Ish spots shortly after leaving his house for the first time after his illness

❋

"Here and there he saw bodies, but in general he found only emptiness."
Narrator describing Ish's journey into town after he first emerges from his cabin

❋

"Men go and come, but earth abides."
The opening quote of the book taken from a passage in Ecclesiastes 1:4 in the Bible. The book was named after this passage.

Endgame

(1957)

WRITTEN BY Samuel Beckett
COUNTRY OF ORIGIN France

Hamm's trashy father and mother, Nagg and Nell, in a performance of *Endgame*.

This absurdist one-act play is set in a gloomy room with two windows—one called "Sea" and the other, "Earth." Inside the room are four characters: a blind, mean-spirited man named Hamm who is confined to a chair; his servant, Clov, on whom he's utterly dependent; and Hamm's parents, Nagg and Nell, who have both lost their legs and now live in trash cans. The play starts with Clov saying, "Finished, it's finished, nearly finished, it must be nearly finished," an expression that gets repeated a few times throughout, in different ways. Though the dialog of the play is abstract, we get the sense that these miserable four are the last humans on earth—and that now their time on the planet is coming to a close.

Throughout the play, Hamm barks orders at Clov and requests his painkillers. Clov repeatedly threatens to leave even though he admits that there is nowhere else to go. Meanwhile, Hamm's elderly parents reminisce about the good old days before they were stuck in dustbins filled with sand and had to live under their awful son's watch.

More Plays Directed by Samuel Beckett
Malone Dies (first published in French, 1951)
Waiting for Godot (first published in French, 1952)
Krapp's Last Tape (1958)
Happy Days (1961)

Clov tries to maintain a sense of normalcy by opening the windows in the morning, planting seeds, and creating a toy dog. But the windows gaze out on an unchanging grey sky, his seeds do not sprout, and the toy dog is a poor excuse for a pet. As all of this is happening, there is a loud clock ticking, and, finally, at the end, Hamm gives a long speech, preparing to die.

💡 The Inspiration

Many believe that Beckett's play was inspired by the fear of nuclear war that existed during the Cold War. The Cold War was basically a standoff between the Communist Soviet Union and the Democratic United States and its allies. It was termed the Cold War because there were no actual attacks on anyone, just a feeling of hostility between the countries based on their political differences. That said, both the Soviet Union and the United States had nuclear weapons in their possession, and people often feared that one or both of the superpowers might use the weapons to cause mass destruction. The Cold War lasted from the end of World War II (mid-1940s) until the end of 1991, when the Soviet Union was dissolved and became the more democratic Russia.

Another more obvious inspiration for the play was the game of chess: The word "endgame" is used in chess to designate the last, very predictable, stage of a game.

🔍 REALITY FACTOR

Since the cause of the apocalypse in *Endgame* is never truly divulged, it's hard to offer a reality factor. On a more literal level, however, there are probably lots of people who feel like they are trapped in miserable circumstances that they can't escape.

⚠ The Impact

✳ *Endgame* was notable for being part of that era's burgeoning absurdist movement. Though Samuel Beckett was of Irish origin, he lived in France for a long time and was a member of the French theatrical movement called the Theatre of the Absurd. This type of theater dealt with themes of confusion and wonder before the unexplainable aspects of our universe, and often incorporated both tragedy and comedy. *Endgame*, which was originally written in French but then translated to English by the bilingual Beckett, became known as a prime example of this type of theatre.

✴ *Endgame* **became known as an important work.** Though the first productions of Endgame weren't especially well-received, it eventually became recognized as an important work after a famous 1964 Parisian production starring Patrick Magee and Jack MacGowran.

✴ **Beckett was awarded the 1969 Nobel Prize in Literature.** He did not win for a specific piece of work, but his theater pieces were noted.

QUOTABLES

Hamm: *Nature has forgotten us.*
Clov: *There's no more nature.*
Hamm and Clov reflecting on the utter lack of anything natural in their lives

✴

Hamm: *I was never there.*
Clov: *Lucky for you.*
Hamm: *Absent always. It all happened without me.*
I don't know what's happened.
Hamm says this toward the end of the play, musing about how quickly time (and life) passes by

 **Eve of Destruction**

(1965)

PERFORMED BY Barry McGuire
WRITTEN BY P. F. Sloan
COUNTRY OF ORIGIN USA

❝ Eve of Destruction" was first recorded by the LA folk-rock act The Turtles, but it was the gruff-voiced Barry McGuire who brought the song some much deserved attention in 1965. It's a classic '60s protest song that talks about the horrors of the era, and it criticizes people for just going around pretending that everything is fine while wars are raging and death is everywhere. The song implies that while people are saying it is the Age of the Aquarius (an age of love and peace), it is actually the "eve of the apocalypse."

The song references many of the most frightening and confusing political events of the mid-'60s, including Bloody Sunday in Selma, Alabama (a Sunday during the civil rights movement in which nonviolent protesters were attacked by local authorities with billy clubs and tear gas); the growing threat of nuclear war between the US and the USSR; the deadly Vietnam War that was taking thousands of American and Vietnamese lives; the Kennedy

Barry McGuire, singer of "Eve of Destruction," belts one out for TV audiences in 1965.

More Songs by Barry McGuire
"Sloop John B" (1965)
"Child of Our Times" (1965)
"Masters of War" (1967)

👁 UNFORGETTABLE MOMENT

After the song's narrator has listed some of his evidence that society is breaking down, he punctuates his message with "If the button is pushed, there's no runnin' away / There'll be no one to save, with the world in a grave." This is about the threat of nuclear destruction — which was just a button-push away at any moment during the Cold War. The singer is reminding his audience that hiding your head in the sand isn't a good survival strategy if the sand is vaporized by a ten-megaton thermonuclear weapon.

assassination; and strife in the Middle East between Israel and Jordan. The line "You may leave here for four days in space / But when you return, it's the same old place" refers to that summer's Gemini 4 mission that took astronauts to space for four days. The point of the song's writer, P.F. Sloan is that, for all its amazing technological advances, the United States couldn't save itself from senseless violence at home and abroad. The song's narrator is most upset, however, that more Americans don't see what he does: a world gone mad, on "the eve of destruction."

🔍 REALITY FACTOR

"Eve of Destruction" doesn't just focus on one path to annihilation, it mentions different ways the world seems to be coming to a close. The largest focus here, though, is on nuclear war. And the probability that the world (or much of the world) would fall apart if nuclear war did break out is relatively high.

💡 The Inspiration

The inspiration was the era in which the song was written. The '60s was a time of tremendous social upheaval. It wasn't all bad—it led to greater civil rights for women and African Americans—but there was also a lot of war and general discord. Many considered "Eve of Destruction" to be a "protest song"—a piece of music designed to express disapproval for something political or social going on in the world. This particular song showed the songwriter's disdain for just about everything going on during this time period.

⚠ The Impact

❋ **The song was banned by some radio stations in the United States and was placed on "restricted play" in Britain.** The stations seemed to think its antiwar message was too radical. Still, the song reached #1 on the Billboard Hot 100 chart in September of 1965.

❋ **The song's message is so poignant that other musicians have continuously re-recorded the song.** Hot Tuna also recorded a version; in the '70s it was punk acts The Dickies; and in the '80s it was Johnny Thunders. In 2008 English rockers The Pogues also released a version. More recently reggae singer Luciano put out a version, and indie rockers Bishop Allen released a song with the same title and snippets of the same lyrics.

❋ **The lyric "You're old enough to kill, but not for votin'" hit home with listeners.** In 1971 the twenty-sixth Amendment lowered all states' voting ages from twenty-one to eighteen—the same age at which an American male could be drafted into war.

⚡ QUOTABLES ⚡

"You're old enough to kill, but not for votin'..."

This lyric points to the fact that the many of the men who were drafted to serve in the Vietnam war were between the ages of eighteen and twenty—under the legal voting age at the time. Hence, these young men were old enough to be drafted and kill people, but not old enough to vote in their own country.

art The Four Horsemen of the Apocalypse
(ca. 1498)

CREATED BY Albrecht Dürer
COUNTRY OF ORIGIN Germany

This woodcut print by influential German artist Albrecht Dürer depicts a key scene from the Book of Revelation (the last book of the King James version of the Bible). Dürer illustrates the opening of four of the seven "seals" from a scroll that holds the final judgment of God. With each seal removed from the scroll, a horseman with a different power is released. From left to right, they are Death, Famine, War, and Plague (or Pestilence).

In the lower-left-hand corner, Death sweeps the citizens into the mouth of hell. The first man to be swallowed up appears to be wearing a crown, which speaks to the Revelation's condemnation of those who misuse their power. The others look resigned to their fate as the horsemen charge on with hollow righteousness in their eyes. An angel hovers above the scene, nested in the clouds of heaven with an almost amused look.

It's just another day in the office for Pestilence, War, Famine, and Death in Albrecht Dürer's *The Four Horsemen of the Apocalypse*.

More Art Created by Albrecht Dürer
Saint Eustace (ca. 1501)
Adam and Eve (1504)
Knight, Death, and the Devil (1513)

Dürer's *The Four Horsemen of the Apocalypse* is the most famous of fifteen woodcuts from the artist's self-published series on the apocalypse. It was printed as a book in 1498, when there was a lot of religious hysteria regarding the possibility that the Last Judgment could occur in 1500. In this series, Dürer not only explored the widespread emotions of fear and angst, but also seemed to consider the extent to which his art could even begin to express themes from the New Testament.

℞EALITY FACTOR

Given the variety of the predictions that Dürer's piece represents, at least one of the maladies behind those four horsemen could lead to humankind's end (famine, for instance, *could* strike the planet, or a massive world war *could* be sparked). But it's highly unlikely that Death, Famine, War, *and* Plague, working together, would sweep humans from the face of the planet. It's just a lot to ask.

💡 The Inspiration

This piece was inspired by a passage in the Book of Revelation (6:1–8): "And I saw, and behold, a white horse, and its rider had a bow; and a crown was given to him, and he went out conquering and to conquer. When he opened the second seal, I heard the second living creature say, 'Come!' And out came another horse, bright red; its rider was permitted to take peace from the earth, so that men should slay one another; and he was given a great sword. When he opened the third seal, I heard the third living creature say, 'Come!' And I saw, and behold, a black horse, and its rider had a balance in his hand. And when he opened the fourth seal, I heard the voice of the fourth living creature say, 'Come!' And I saw, and behold, a pale horse, and its rider's name was Death, and Hades followed him."

⚠ The Impact

＊ **Dürer's self-published "Apocalypse" series established him as a successful working artist.** He had intended to use print-making as his primary source of income, but the fame that he achieved as a result of this particular series (published only three years after he opened his workshop) allowed him to achieve success as a professional artist.

＊ **_The Four Horsemen_ influenced many other artists.** The French artist Odilon Redon (1840–1916) seemed inspired by Dürer's work in his twelve-lithograph series "Apocalypse de Saint-Jean" (1899). Dürer's piece also influenced contemporary artist Gordon Cheung, whose 2009 solo exhibition, _The Four Horsemen of the Apocalypse_, included laser etchings based on Durer's woodcut.

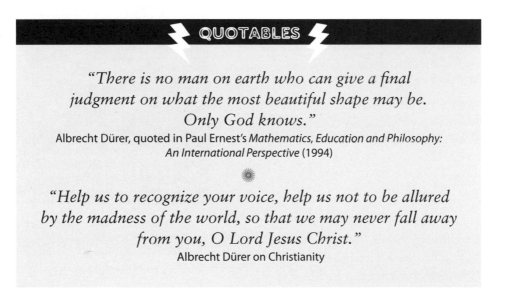

⚡ QUOTABLES ⚡

"There is no man on earth who can give a final judgment on what the most beautiful shape may be. Only God knows."
Albrecht Dürer, quoted in Paul Ernest's _Mathematics, Education and Philosophy: An International Perspective_ (1994)

✳

"Help us to recognize your voice, help us not to be allured by the madness of the world, so that we may never fall away from you, O Lord Jesus Christ."
Albrecht Dürer on Christianity

Gimme Shelter

(1969)

PERFORMED BY The Rolling Stones
WRITTEN BY Mick Jagger and Keith Richards
COUNTRY OF ORIGIN England

Mick Jagger performing with the Rolling Stones at the height of their popularity (and very bad behavior).

In "Gimme Shelter," one of the best songs by the legendary rock group The Rolling Stones, singer Mick Jagger's trademark voice captures a dark moment at the tail end of the '60s. During that time, the movement for peace and love seemed to be overtaken by drugs, war, and violence. The song's dire chorus, "Rape, murder / it's just a shot away," captures the sense that terrible forces have been unleashed and that shelter is both necessary and elusive. The music itself—threatening and ominous—sets the mood as much as the howl of the lyrics, which are only half-intelligible and blend into the overall sense of menace and breakdown.

The song starts out with Mick Jagger singing that a building storm is threatening his life, and that if he doesn't find shelter, he's "gonna fade away." He then launches into the chorus, imploring listening "children" to understand and acknowledge that war is right around the corner. The apocalyptic

More Songs Written and Performed by The Rolling Stones

"(I Can't Get No) Satisfaction " (1965)

"Sympathy For The Devil" (1968)

"You Can't Always Get What You Want" (1969)

imagery builds as Jagger describes a huge fire, like a "red coal carpet," and then likens it to a crazed, violent bull. Jagger then describes a world descending into chaos, and again reminds us that the end—large-scale destruction—is "just a shot away." Toward the end of the song, though, Jagger changes his tune a bit and asks us to remember that, though war may only be a gunshot away, love and peace are "just a kiss away," too.

ℝEALITY FACTOR

The lyrics cover a broad swath of apocalyptic themes: everything from rape and murder to fire, floods, and wartime gunshots. Much of the imagery feels very realistic, but the chances of all of these things happening at once in a kind of apocalyptic superstorm is slim. However, it's certainly possible, in hard times, to *feel* like everything is falling apart all at once and bringing the world to an end.

💡 The Inspiration

Mick Jagger and Keith Richards (who co-wrote "Gimme Shelter") intended for the song and the entire *Let It Bleed* album to capture the sense of impending doom and apocalyptic social disintegration that was in the air at the time. In a 1995 interview with *Rolling Stone*, Jagger explained that the band's inspiration for the album was the Vietnam War and the generally violent overtones of the era.

⚠ The Impact

✳ **"Gimme Shelter" became notorious at the famous Altamont concert.** The day after their album *Let It Bleed* was released in 1969, The Rolling Stones were part of a famous free concert at the Altamont Speedway in Altamont, California. Unlike the Woodstock concert four months earlier, which was all about love and peace, this music festival was marked by fighting, property damage, drug use, and death. While the Stones were playing "Under My Thumb" on stage, a homicide occurred in which a guy from the Hell's Angels (a motorcycle gang that was hired to provide security at the concert) stabbed and killed a fan who was high on methamphetamines and seemed to be holding a gun. After working to calm the generally uneasy crowd, the Stones, uninformed about the murder, played eight more songs, including "Gimme Shelter." The song has been linked with the event (and the whole atmosphere of the time) ever since. *Gimme Shelter* was also the name for a famous documentary about the band's 1969 tour, and its tragic climax at Altamont.

✳ **Martin Scorsese has featured the song in several of his gangster films.** He tends to use the song to signal the beginning of a character's violent downfall—check out *Casino* (1995), *Goodfellas* (1990), and *The Departed* (2006).

✳ **The song has historical import.** It was ranked at #38 on *Rolling Stone* magazine's list of the 500 Greatest Songs of All Time.

QUOTABLES

"Ooh, see the fire is sweepin' / My very street today / Burns like a red coal carpet / Mad bull lost its way."
The portion of the song where Jagger likens the late '60's turbulence to a fire and a raging bull

I Am Legend (1954)

WRITTEN BY Richard Matheson

COUNTRY OF ORIGIN USA

I Am Legend is one of the first modern vampire novels. In it, a terrible virus has infected humankind, turning everyone on the planet into vampires—except for a man named Robert Neville. As the sole survivor of this epidemic, Neville, who lost a wife and daughter to the vampire virus, has become depressed and has resigned himself to the life of a solitary, heavy-drinking shut-in. His days and nights follow the same endless pattern. He gets up, makes breakfast, and then sets about his daily vampire-prevention tasks: stringing up wreaths of garlic, boarding up all his windows, and taking dead vampire corpses to burn in a fire pit. Because the vampires only go out at night, Neville is free to roam the deserted city by day, picking up supplies from stores (for free, of course), and developing various ways (including a blood test) to distinguish a vampire from a human, should he ever again come across one. But at night he's focused on fending off the swarms of vamps that lurk outside his house.

Will Smith thought about driving across the bridge pictured in this *I Am Legend* movie poster, but then decided against it.

More Books Written by Richard Matheson

The Incredible Shrinking Man (1956)

Hell House (1971)

What Dreams May Come (1978)

👁 UNFORGETTABLE MOMENT

In Ruth's note, she explains that she and a community of other vampires are organizing to form a new society, and vampires are poised to take over the world. It's in this moment that Neville loses any remaining glimmer of hope and realizes he is truly the last man standing.

Then, one day, he meets a woman called Ruth (named after author Richard Matheson's real-life wife), who appears to be human. They spend some time together and Neville asks if she will take the blood test. She doesn't want to (she says she's afraid of the result), but she eventually gives in, as he promises that he will find a cure if the result is positive. Right as the test proves she is positive, Ruth clubs Neville over the head. When he wakes up, he finds a note from her, explaining that she's part of a new community of diseased vampires that have managed to adapt and that can now tolerate sunlight for short periods of time. As the last member of the "old society," Neville is in danger, because the new vampire community hates him for killing their own. Ruth's note stresses that Neville should leave town, but he's too depressed to leave. Soon, vampires show up and drag him away to their lair. While awaiting his execution, Neville realizes he is the true outsider. There's a new society, where infection is normal, and he's now going to be nothing more than a "legend."

💡 The Inspiration

Author Richard Matheson got the idea for *I Am Legend* after watching the 1931 movie *Dracula* starring Bela Lugosi. Matheson has stated that he thought a "whole world" of vampires would be even scarier than a story about just one vampire.

⚠️ The Impact

* *I Am Legend* played a big part in the developing popularity of the zombie genre. The novel was brought to life on the big screen three separate times: in *The Last Man on Earth* (1964), *The Omega Man*

🔍 REALITY FACTOR

This one is easy. Vampires aren't real. So the idea of a blood-sucker apocalypse (or even a vampire virus) isn't possible. Sorry, Twi-hards.

(1971), and *I Am Legend* (2007), pictured on page 77, starring Will Smith. George A. Romero admits to having been strongly influenced by Matheson's book for his 1968 film *Night of the Living Dead* (page 107), which really brought zombies into the limelight.

*The book had a big influence on other big-name horror masters.** Author Stephen King has said that Matheson is the writer who influenced him the most, and director Steven Spielberg got his first big break with Matheson's script for *Duel*. Modern day best-selling horror author Dean Koontz has also praised Matheson's work.

⚡ QUOTABLES ⚡

Full circle. A new terror born in death, a new superstition entering the unassailable fortress of forever. I am legend.

Neville thinks this to himself in the last lines of the book as he dies at the hands of the vampires

✹

"Come out, Neville!"

Neville's neighbor and friend, Ben Cortman, who's now a vampire, says this. He spends every night outside Neville's house calling his name, begging for him to emerge

✹

"But sooner or later we'll be too well organized, and nothing I say will stop the rest from destroying you. For God's sake, Robert, go now, while you can!"

A passage from the note Ruth leaves for Neville, in which she warns him to leave town as fast as he can

Invasion of the Body Snatchers (1956)

DIRECTED BY Don Siegel

WRITTEN BY Daniel Mainwaring and Jack Finney

COUNTRY OF ORIGIN USA

Dr. Miles Bennell (Kevin McCarthy) will think twice about eating peas after his run-in with a pod in _Invasion of the Body Snatchers_.

Invasion of the Body Snatchers is set in a fictional California town called Santa Mira, where some very strange things are happening. People in the town have begun complaining to the local doctor, Miles J. Bennell (Kevin McCarthy), that their loved ones seem like impostors; Dr. Bennell's former flame, a Liz Taylor lookalike named Becky Driscoll (Dana Wynter), tells him that her cousin Wilma (Virginia Christine) is convinced that something similar is going on with her uncle Ira. As a result, Dr. Bennell and Becky head to Wilma's home to talk with her. There, Dr. Bennell has a conversation with Ira, and finds him to be his usual self. But Wilma is convinced that there's something not right about him. She says that he looks, talks,

and acts the same as regular old Uncle Ira, but there's no feeling in his eyes. Dr. Bennell urges her to see a psychiatrist, and leaves.

Later that night, the doctor is at dinner with Becky when he's called to the home of Jack (King Donovan) and Teddy Belicec (Carolyn Jones). They've found the lifeless body of a man who looks like Jack. Later that night,

More Directed by Don Siegel
Dirty Harry (1971)
The Shootist (1976)
Escape From Alcatraz (1979)

👁 UNFORGETTABLE MOMENT

When Dr. Bennell reaches the height of desperation and fear, he runs into traffic to warn oncoming drivers about the pod transformations. Then, looking absolutely crazed, he stares directly into the camera as he yells, "They're already here! You're next! *You're next!*"

Dr. Bennell finds a similar replica of Becky in her father's basement, and then stumbles upon a few more bodies as they're "born" from oversized pod-like shells covered in sappy foam. He realizes these pod creatures are replacing the real humans they resemble, and the transformations are sweeping through their town.

Dr. Bennell and Becky hole up in his office. Realizing that the pods are most effective at replacing people when they're asleep, the twosome take pills to keep awake. The next morning some friends arrive and admit that they, too, have been turned into pods. They say the pods are from outer space, and that soon everyone on Earth will be turned into pod people, unable to experience human emotions like hate and love. Eventually Becky falls asleep for just a moment, which is all it takes for her to be replaced by a pod person. With the creatures on his trail, Dr. Bennell runs onto the highway, screaming about the alien invasion. Dr. Bennell is finally picked up by the cops and questioned, but they don't believe his account … until they learn of an accident involving a truck full of strange-looking giant seed pods.

🔍 REALITY FACTOR

There's really nothing realistic about this film. The threat of all humans being replaced, in their sleep, by bizarre frothy alien pod replicas is, well, pretty implausible.

💡 The Inspiration

The film was based on the novel *The Body Snatchers* by Jack Finney, which was originally serialized in *Collier's* magazine in 1954.

⚠️ The Impact

✳ **The film became known throughout the world.** Its name is used in casual conservations to describe when something very disturbing appears to be happening just below the surface of normal, everyday life. For instance, in March 2011, Chris

Matthews said he thought the Tea Party's influence on the Republican party was like *Invasion of the Body Snatchers*. In other words, he thought formerly smart Republicans were having their bodies "snatched," leaving behind zombies who mindlessly adopted uber-right-wing positions.

✴ **It's believed that the film was written as an indictment of McCarthyism.** Throughout the Cold War, in the 1940s and 1950s, America was consumed with anxiety about the perceived threat of communism in America. Taking advantage of those fears, Senator Joseph McCarthy made a public accusation that more than two hundred "card-carrying" Communists had broken into the US government. Some people believe *Invasion of the Body Snatchers* uses the pod people's attempts to take over humanity as a symbol of the effects of mass hysteria, which festered during McCarthyism. Walter Mirisch, the producer who supervised the movie, has denied this.

QUOTABLES

"There's no emotion. None. Just the pretense of it. The words, gesture, the tone of voice—everything else is the same, but not the feeling."

Becky's cousin Wilma talking to Dr. Bennell about her "new" Uncle Ira

"In my practice, I've seen how people have allowed their humanity to drain away. Only, it happened slowly instead of all at once ... All of us, a little bit, we harden our hearts and grow callous. Only when we have to fight to stay human do we realize how precious it is to us, how dear."

Dr. Bennell talking to Becky as they are hiding out in his office

🎵 song "It's The End Of The World As We Know It (And I Feel Fine)" (1987)

WRITTEN AND PERFORMED BY
R.E.M.

COUNTRY OR ORIGIN USA

Aside from making hit records, R.E.M. likes nothing better than just standing on a hill and pointing.

❝ It's The End Of The World As We Know It (And I Feel Fine)" was an uber-popular hit song by 1980s–2000s alt-rock band R.E.M. It was first released on the band's 1987 album Document, and was later featured on two R.E.M. compilation albums (Eponymous and And I Feel Fine … The Best of the I.R.S. Years 1982–1987).

The song is four minutes of semi-nonsensical end-of-world references, from natural disasters to manmade threats. But it has such a bouncy beat—and the lyrics are sung in such a fast, stream-of-consciousness style—that many R.E.M. fans just bust out silly dance moves whenever the song comes on, barely noticing the apocalyptic references.

In addition to all of the references to things falling apart, which include "wire in a fire," "continental drift divide," and "book-burning, blood-letting," lead singer Michael Stipe also randomly calls out a mini-list of individuals with the initials

More Songs by R.E.M
"Stand" (1988)
"Losing My Religion" (1991)
"Everybody Hurts" (1992)

👁 UNFORGETTABLE MOMENT

The most unforgettable moment in the song, of course, is when Stipe declares in the chorus that "it's the end of the world as we know it." On the bright side, the next thing he says is "and I feel fine."

L.B. (Leonard Bernstein, Leonid Brezhnev, Lenny Bruce and Lester Bangs). This also doesn't entirely make sense but, again, fans love it all the same.

ℝ EALITY FACTOR

Stipe rattles off a zillion ways the world could end in the first minute of the song alone. OK, maybe not a zillion—but there are about nineteen different references to death and disaster, including earthquakes, "birds and snakes," airplanes, continental drift, knives, fire, and, in different parts of the song, mentions of a "low plane" and "foreign towers" (which feels a bit eerie in a post-9/11 context). Though fires, attack birds, and knives are all fairly common things, it's not so likely that we'd be attacked by them all at once and die out as a species. Then again, the song's title is "It's The End of the World As We Know It," which could simply be referencing the changing of times rather than the world literally coming to an end.

💡 The Inspiration

R.E.M. guitarist Peter Buck has indicated that "End of the World" was influenced by the political "chaos" going on in the United States during 1987. Specifically, Buck mentioned being freaked out by the preaching of right-wing "moralists" (he was referring to President Ronald Reagan and his followers), and Reagan's "jokes" about bombing Russia.

The L.B. references came from a dream Stipe had in which he found himself at a party where he was the only guest who didn't have these shared initials. Stipe once said that this dream showed him that he was a "walking phone book."

⚠ The Impact

✳ **It was a low-ranking hit.** The song didn't make it to the top of any billboard charts, but it still became one of R.E.M.'s most ubiquitous songs. Everyone knows it.

✳ **Its cultural influence has been far-reaching.** The song was featured in the opening moments of the 1996 blockbuster movie *Independence Day*, made an appearance in the comic strip "Pearls Before Swine"

in 2007, and served as the title for a pair of *Grey's Anatomy* episodes in 2005 (one was called "It's the End of the World" and the other was called "As We Know It").

✳ **It became the song for WENZ.** It was played on a twenty-four-hour loop by Cleveland, Ohio, radio station WENZ as a publicity stunt when the station's format was changed to alternative-rock and it was renamed 107.9 The END.

⚡ QUOTABLES ⚡

"That's great, it starts with an earthquake, birds and snakes, an aeroplane — Lenny Bruce is not afraid."

First lyric of the song, which begins to list various weird causes of an apocalypse. Lenny Bruce was a controversial comedian from the 1960s who is famous for having been tried for "obscenity" charges back when it was illegal for public performers to make lewd comments. He was often seen as fearless. (Bruce is also simply a guy with the initials L.B. — see Inspiration.)

Jeremiah
(2002–2004)

CREATED BY J. Michael Straczynski
COUNTRY OF ORIGIN USA

Kurdy (Malcolm Jamal Warner) challenges Jeremiah (Luke Perry) to a staring contest in *Jeremiah*.

Showtime's short-lived TV series *Jeremiah* begins fifteen years after a plague called The Big Death has killed off everyone in the world who had gone through puberty, leaving a civilization of children behind. The show is set in 2021, and the children who had survived the deadly virus have grown into adults who find themselves at a crossroads: Should they continue surviving off the scraps of yesterday, or should they try to create a new world and a new future from the ground up? Meanwhile, there is the constant fear of the plague returning in an even more virulent form.

During the course of the show's two seasons, the main character, Jeremiah (Luke Perry), a heroic and very moral kid, searches for his father, a viral scientist he believes may still be alive in a mysterious and mythic refuge called Valhalla Sector. During a random stop in Colorado, Jeremiah teams up with fellow wandering loner Kurdy Molloy (Malcolm-Jamal Warner), who becomes his cynical sidekick. The duo hears about a colony, Thunder Mountain, comprised of children (now young adults) spared by The Big Death.

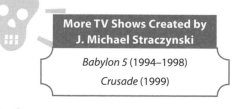

**More TV Shows Created by
J. Michael Straczynski**

Babylon 5 (1994–1998)

Crusade (1999)

👁 UNFORGETTABLE MOMENT

Early in the show's first episode, we see—via a flashback—Jeremiah's parents leave the children behind to go look for a supposed refuge in Valhalla Sector. Jeremiah's mom says they'll be back in "less than an hour." Jeremiah later finds his mother's dead body outside.

Thunder Mountain is significant not only because it has information related to Valhalla Sector, but also because its leader, Markus Alexander (Peter Stebbings), has all the resources necessary to start society anew. As Jeremiah and Kurdy make their way toward Thunder Mountain, they encouter all kinds of strange and fascinating characters and places, including a whole town dead from cyanide; a mysterious group called the Burners that's been burning down entire settlements; and a town called New Hope whose inhabitants aren't allowed to touch anyone (and are punished for disobeying the rule). They even uncover an isolated contingent of Black Power enthusiasts. Markus and Jeremiah eventually learn that there's a vaccine for The Big Death—and that a man named Lee Smith plans to release the virus again. They must now try to get the vaccine and stop the rerelease of the virus.

💡 The Inspiration

Jeremiah is an adaptation of an award-winning European graphic novel series by Hermann Huppen, which was originally launched in 1979.

ⓡ EALITY FACTOR

The population-killer here is a plague called The Big Death, which seems to have hit suddenly and killed anyone past the age of puberty. While the likelihood of a pandemic striking the globe is fairly high, the likelihood of one that discriminates against adults and spares the children is pretty low.

⚠ The Impact

* **It became a cult classic.** Though *Jeremiah* didn't get a ton of press or critical acclaim, it became a fan favorite—and its popularity wasn't just thanks to Perry's pretty face. In fact, fans freaked out when Showtime announced that *Jeremiah*'s second season (already underway) would be its last. Eight additional episodes of the show had apparently already been produced, but Showtime had no plans to air them.

* **It paved the way for other children-running-the-world tales.** Michael Grant's 2009 young adult book *Gone*, for instance, is about a society in which all of the world's adults spontaneously disappear and the children are left to raise themselves.

* **Unlike some other works in the post-apocalyptic genre,** *Jeremiah* **stood out for its relatively unspectacular special effects.** It tended to rely on dialogue and character development instead of action-packed thrills 'n' chills, and developed a unique following for this reason.

QUOTABLES

"Dear Dad, I think about you every day ... six billion lights that went out in six months. Six billion lives lost to a mystery."
Jeremiah narrating a letter he's written to his dad in the opening episode

"The thunder will change you forever. Everyone you love will fall at the end of the world."
Creepy homeless man's vision for Jeremiah, who has already lost everyone he loves, in the opening episode

The Last Judgment (1536–1541)

CREATED BY Michelangelo

COUNTRY OF ORIGIN Vatican City

This terrifying and awe-inspiring painting is located on the altar wall in the Sistine Chapel in Rome, Italy. The Sistine Chapel was commissioned by Pope Sixtus IV in 1475, and was created to be the pope's chapel and the site of papal elections (and it still serves those functions today). The work depicts the Last Judgment—the time when, according to the New Testament, the world will come to an end and all humans will be judged by God. In the painting, masses of naked humans rise from the Earth to be judged by Jesus, who is sitting above them on a throne surrounded by saints. Muscular, wingless angels hover above as well, sounding the trumpets of Revelation, calling souls to rise to judgment. Demons claw at the damned and drag them down, while more angels guide the saved upward.

It's a no-pants kind of day for everyone in Michaelangelo's *The Last Judgment* at the Sistine Chapel in Rome.

More Art Created by Michelangelo

David (sculpture, 1504)

Sistine Chapel ceiling
(painting, 1508–1512)

St. Peter's Basilica (architect; completed 1626)

Paintings depicting Judgment Day—also known as Dooms—were very popular as church decoration during Michelangelo's time. They were usually given prominent placement to better help parishioners ponder their mortality and their levels of sinfulness. *The Last Judgment* is probably the most famous Doom today, and it shares many features with other Dooms, including the inclusion of St. John the Evangelist; a focus on Jesus, with Mary at his side; and souls rising to meet their judgment (and falling into hell when they're found lacking). This work also depicts St. Bartholomew, a martyr who was skinned alive. He's shown holding his empty skin, but Michelangelo painted his own face onto it! Despite its similarities to a lot of other Dooms, Michelangelo's painting had an important difference in that it depicted the people without clothes, thus stripping them of identifying details like social class or occupation.

REALITY FACTOR

The painting is most closely linked with the predictions about Judgment Day that were included in the Book of Revelation, but it also borrows from Dante's visions of Hell in *The Inferno*, from around 1314. Judgment Day—which changes from one version of Christianity to another—is generally supposed to occur at some point in the future, and be part of a series of events including the resurrection of the dead, the second coming of Christ, and various plagues and wars. Can it really happen? That all depends on whether or not you believe in this section of the Bible.

The Inspiration

Twenty-six years earlier Michelangelo had painted the ceiling of the Sistine Chapel, which became a huge, beautiful painting featuring many intricate scenes from the Bible. In 1534, Pope Clement VII commissioned him to return to paint a resurrection scene behind the altar, but then the Pope died shortly afterward. Clement's successor, Pope Paul III, felt a Judgment Day scene would be more fitting for the mood of Rome at the time, and asked Michelangelo to change course. Pope Paul III may have had a point. Rome had recently faced several huge obstacles and setbacks: The sack of Rome in 1527 (a military action against the Catholic Church by the armies of the Holy Roman Emperor, Charles V) had destroyed thousands of churches, palaces, and houses, and the Catholic church was also busy fighting the Protestant Reformation, a sixteenth-century European movement that strove to reshape the beliefs and actions of the Roman Catholic Church.

⚠ The Impact

✳ **The work was considered scandalous at the time.** Church leaders were distraught by all the naughty bits, and deemed the work more fit for a tavern than a church in the Vatican. Eventually they hired one of Michelangelo's own students to add drapery, loincloths, and other obscur-ing devices to the people in the painting. Some of the coverings were removed later during a restoration of the artwork.

✳ **The work is one of the most treasured artworks in the world.** Four million people visit the Sistine Chapel each year, many of them solely to behold Michelangelo's works.

The Last Man (1826)

WRITTEN BY Mary Wollstonecraft Shelley
COUNTRY OF ORIGIN England

Set in an apocalyptic future between 2073 and 2100 AD, Shelley's long three-volume novel depicts a plague that destroys almost all of humankind. The novel opens with Shelley claiming that during an 1818 trip to Naples, she discovered a collection of prophetic writings about the end of the world painted on leaves in a cave. She writes that she compiled these writings into *The Last Man*—an (obviously fictional) account of the last person alive at the end of the twenty-first century.

Set in England, the book focuses on a complex array of characters living interwoven and somewhat tragic lives. The last man is a shepherd named Lionel Verney. Other important figures include Adrian, the former crown prince of England; Lionel's sister, Perdita; and her lover, Lord Raymond, the newly elected Lord Protector of England.

Lord Raymond renounces his position and leads a military campaign in Greece to reestablish independence and overthrow the Turkish Empire. Then a horrific plague

Mary Wollstonecraft Shelley, the author of *The Last Man* (and *Frankenstein*) ca. 1840.

More Books Written by Mary Shelley

Frankenstein, or *The Modern Prometheus* (1818)

The Fortunes of Perkin Warbeck, A Romance (three volumes, 1830)

The book's most crucial moment is toward the end, when Adrian and Clara drown, leaving Lionel Verney alone as the last man on earth.

begins to spread all over the world, slowly creeping toward England and killing almost everyone in its wake.

Lionel and Adrian struggle to stay alive and save the human race. With two others, they escape to Switzerland, where they hope (oddly enough) that a colder climate may protect them against the disease. The plague eventually runs its course and ends, but one of the foursome dies of fever. Two more drown during a storm en route to Greece, leaving Lionel standing alone as the last man.

® EALITY FACTOR

Shelley's book is unique in that it's set far in the future, yet she describes virtually zero technological or scientific advances. It's almost laughable, really, how similar the future in *The Last Man* actually looks to the 1820s, when Shelley wrote the book. Though there is always a possibility that a new type of virus could develop and start sweeping the world (remember swine flu?), it's not feasible that there would be no technological or medical advances in place to help offset the destruction.

💡 The Inspiration

It's widely believed that the main characters from *The Last Man* were based on Shelley's nearest and dearest. The character Adrian was supposedly based on her late husband, Percy Shelley, who is portrayed as both a courageous idealist and an egocentric narcissist. She wrote the book while still grieving the 1822 death of her famous husband; three of the couple's children had also died, soon after being born.

⚠ The Impact

✳ **Shelley's apocalyptic vision paved the way for many authors to come.** Though not the very first "last man on Earth" book, Shelley's was one of the earliest novels to explore the concept. And the author's plot line—apocalyptic plague destroys society and the human race—was copied by many future authors. Examples include *The Scarlet Plague* (see page 116; 1912), *Earth Abides* (page 62; 1949), and *The Stand* (page 125; 1978).

✳ **The writer used a technique that would go on to become common in literature.** Shelley wrote from the perspective of a present-day narrator who hears the story secondhand. In this case, at the beginning of the series, the author describes a visit to Naples, where she discovered ancient prophecies written inside a cave. It's these writings that Shelley claims to turn into *The Last Man*.

⚡ QUOTABLES ⚡

"The day passed thus; each moment contained eternity; although when hour after hour had gone by, I wondered at the quick flight of time. Yet even now I had not drunk the bitter potion to the dregs; I was not yet persuaded of my loss; I did not yet feel in every pulsation, in every nerve, in every thought, that I remained alone of my race—that I was the LAST MAN."

Lionel's reaction to the death of Clara and Adrian

※

"The dead were carried out, and the sick brought in, with like indifference; some were screaming with pain, others laughing from the influence of more terrible delerium; some were attended by weeping, despairing relations, others called aloud with thrilling tenderness or reproach on the friends who had deserted them while the nurses went from bed to bed, incarnate images of despair, neglect, and death."

The narrator's rather explicit description of the suffering of plague victims

Logan's Run

(1976)

DIRECTED BY Michael Anderson

WRITTEN BY David Zelag Goodman, William F. Nolan, and George Clayton Johnson

COUNTRY OF ORIGIN USA

There's nowhere to go but up for these Carrousel participants in *Logan's Run*. (Happy vaporizing!)

Logan's Run is a film set in the year 2274. An unnamed catastrophe in the distant past has forced people to live in a dome-enclosed city, where they are monitored by a monolithic master computer. People appear to be happy with their otherwise carefree existences though. No one works or gets married, and there are "orgy rooms" where people go to have sex and do drugs. However, this new society has one major drawback: To maintain population control and the balance of their resources, everyone is forced to die when they turn thirty in a bizarre ceremony known as Carrousel. People are told that, if they're lucky, they might be "renewed" during the ritual—that is, they'll have a chance to be reincarnated. But as it

happens, all the participants assemble in an arena, where they're lifted up by an unseen force, and then vaporized.

The only way to escape Carrousel is to become a "runner"—someone who tries to escape from society. A special group of police officers (called the Sandmen) is

More Movies Directed by Michael Anderson
Around the World in Eighty Days (1956)
1984 (1956)
Millennium (1989)

👁 UNFORGETTABLE MOMENT

When the computer informs Logan, in an ever-so-nonchalant way, about his mission to find and destroy Sanctuary—a place he had always dismissed as a rumor or an urban myth—it understandably sends Logan for a loop. It's here that his once solid faith in the system begins to crack.

in charge of tracking down runners and bringing them back to be killed. A Sandman named Logan 5 (Michael York) is content with his life and a believer in the system. Then he meets a woman named Jessica (Jenny Agutter), who shares with Logan her fears about dying and her doubts about renewal. She also confesses her desire to reach Sanctuary, a rumored haven for runners that Logan doesn't believe exists. Logan scoffs at her idea, but shortly after their meeting, the computer gives him the assignment of his life:

ℝ EALITY FACTOR

The story is not particularly realistic. We never find out what devastated the world in the first place, and the fact that the world is composed entirely of attractive Caucasian people also seems a bit unlikely.

he must leave the dome, penetrate the outside gates, find Sanctuary, and then destroy all the runners within it. To complete this mission, he must pose as a runner and convince Jessica, whom he has started to fall in love with, to help him find the elusive paradise. As they fight their way out of the city, they discover the truth about Sanctuary and the shattered world outside the dome.

💡 The Inspiration

The movie was based on the 1967 novel of the same name by William F. Nolan and George Clayton Johnson.

⚠ The Impact

✳ **The movie's special effects were considered groundbreaking for their time.** *Logan's Run* won an Oscar for visual effects at the Academy Awards in 1977. The impressive futuristic backdrops were achieved through elaborate matte paintings and miniatures. Unfortunately, *Star Wars* was released the following year, and all other sci-fi movies pretty much paled in comparison to it.

✳ **The film was noted for its complicated stunt work.** The Carrousel ceremony contained one of the most complicated flying wire stunts ever done for a movie. In the scene, people were shown to be drifting upward toward heaven, as if they were being redeemed; some shots had to be filmed upside-down to make the scene work.

✳ **The 1976 movie inspired a remake.** A new version of the film, written by Alex Garland (see *28 Days Later*, page 11) and starring Ryan Gosling is currently said to be in development.

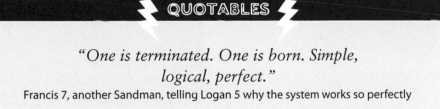

QUOTABLES

"One is terminated. One is born. Simple, logical, perfect."
Francis 7, another Sandman, telling Logan 5 why the system works so perfectly

"Be strong and you will be renewed."
PA system during the opening of a Carrousel ceremony

The Machine Stops (1909)

WRITTEN BY E.M. Forster

COUNTRY OF ORIGIN UK

This futuristic short story opens with a woman, Vashti, sealed up in a small room beneath an island in the southern hemisphere, her walls dotted with buttons and switches. There's a hot bath button, and buttons to call for food, for music, for clothing, and for her bed. Vashti (and the rest of humankind) now lives underground because the surface of the Earth has become uninhabitable. All of the technology at her disposal is run by the Machine, an omnipotent mechanical force that runs, well, everything.

Vashti's son, Kuno, lives far away, beneath the northern hemisphere. She communicates with him (despite the fact that parent-child communication is now illegal), using a "round plate" that glows and shows his image. She also visits him once, upon his insistence, by air ship. When she arrives, she learns that the Machine has threatened to kick Kuno out of his cell and send him to the surface of the Earth to die because

E.M. Forster, the author of "The Machine Stops," after hearing a mildly humorous story.

<table>
<tr><th colspan="2">More Written by E.M. Forster</th></tr>
</table>

More Written by E.M. Forster

Howard's End (novel, 1910)

A Passage to India (novel, 1924)

👁 UNFORGETTABLE MOMENT

Kuno tells his mother about a risky journey he took to the surface of the Earth in which he mentions that he was able to communicate with spirits of the dead and the unborn. These communications have allowed him to see that humanity existed long before the oppressive technology of the Machine.

he ventured there himself once without the Machine's permission. Vashti thinks Kuno has become too much of a rebel and returns home to the comfort of her cell. People become more and more reliant on the

🔍 REALITY FACTOR

We never learn exactly what caused the destruction of life on the Earth's surface or why humans were forced to go underground, so it's hard to say how realistic that aspect of the story is. The story is, however, extraordinarily accurate in its portrayals of future technology. The 1909 story mentions variations on technologies that wouldn't be developed for the masses until far into the future: a video-conferencing-like "speaking apparatus," a television-like "cinematophote," and an "isolation switch" (almost like setting your cell phone to "silent" on a large scale) to shut out the constant barrage of technological interruptions. It also describes, nearly to a T, our modern culture's obsession with virtual communication (email, internet, texting, etc.) and the resulting physical isolation we experience.

Machine daily (they even start to worship it as a god), but it's beginning to break down, and when it finally collapses for good, so does society. Kuno comes to Vashti's ruined cell before they die, and together they realize how society's overreliance on technology has disconnected everyone from what's real in the world.

💡 The Inspiration

Author E. M. Forster wrote, in the introduction to his *Collected Short Stories*, that he intended for "The Machine Stops" to be from a point of view counter to that of H.G. Wells (see *The War of the Worlds*, a radio play based on a novel by Wells, on page 137). Wells's work often took a pro-technology, futuristic stance, and Forster wanted to show the dark side of man's growing enthusiasm for technology.

⚠ The Impact

✳ **"The Machine Stops" has gone down in history.** It was included in *The Science Fiction Hall of Fame, Volume Two B* (1973), and has also inspired thinkers like computer scientist Jaron Lanier (who coined the term "virtual reality" and authored the book *You Are Not a Gadget: A Manifesto).* Lanier has recommended the story to others while promoting his own book.

✳ **It set the stage for later science fiction works about technologically triggered apocalypses.** In Harlan Ellison's 1967 short story "I Have No Mouth & I Must Scream," a supercomputer becomes self-conscious and kills all but five people. Arthur C. Clarke's 1956 novel, *The City and the Stars,* is about an enclosed city run by a machine known as the Central Computer. More modern films like *Logan's Run* (1976, page 95), *The Matrix* (1999), and *WALL-E* (2008, page 134) also touch on similar themes.

✳ **The story was adapted into other forms.** It became an episode of the British TV program *Out of the Unknown* in 1966, was turned into a radio play by playwright Eric Coble in 2007, and was made into a short film by the Freise Brothers in 2009. The band Level 42 also named a song after "The Machine Stops."

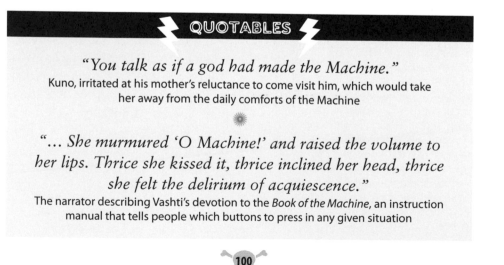

⚡ QUOTABLES ⚡

"You talk as if a god had made the Machine."
Kuno, irritated at his mother's reluctance to come visit him, which would take her away from the daily comforts of the Machine

✳

"… She murmured 'O Machine!' and raised the volume to her lips. Thrice she kissed it, thrice inclined her head, thrice she felt the delirium of acquiescence."
The narrator describing Vashti's devotion to the *Book of the Machine,* an instruction manual that tells people which buttons to press in any given situation

Mad Max 2: The Road Warrior
(1981)

DIRECTED BY George Miller

WRITTEN BY George Miller, Terry Hayes, and Brian Hannant

COUNTRY OF ORIGIN Australia

Mel Gibson needs a good mechanic and a shave in *Mad Max 2: The Road Warrior*.

The second installment in the *Mad Max* film series focuses, once again, on our buff "road warrior" Mad Max Rockatansky (Mel Gibson). While the first *Mad Max* movie centered on Max as he avenged the violent deaths of his wife and child, *The Road Warrior* focuses on the frontier communities that have sprung up in the post-apocalyptic desert landscape.

The film's opening voiceover informs us that the cities have "exploded" and that looting and violence have taken over Australia. Because of a worldwide energy shortage, gas is priced extremely high—it's something people will go to crazy lengths to obtain. The film begins with Max and his loyal cattle dog roaming the desert in search of food and gas. After escaping a group of mohawked marauders led by a character named Wez (Vernon Wells), Max stumbles upon a seemingly abandoned autogyro helicopter. He soon realizes that the aircraft's owner is hiding. He threatens the man (Bruce Spence) until the man offers up some crucial information: There's a small oil refinery nearby.

More Movies Directed by George Miller
The Witches of Eastwick (1987)
Babe: Pig in the City (1998)
Happy Feet (2006)

Max takes the man captive as they seek out the refinery. Once they find it, Max watches on from a nearby cliff as the marauders descend on the refinery and attack the community living there. Soon there is a standoff, and the marauders' leader—a hockey-mask-wearing character known as The Humungus (Kjell Nilsson)—offers a safe exit from the wastelands if the settlers will leave the facility and give up their fuel reserves. Max heads down to the refinery at this point and offers the settlers a deal: in exchange for as much gas as he can carry, Max will bring

back an abandoned Mack truck, so that the settlers can escape with at least some of their fuel. They accept.

The remainder of the film follows Max and the settlers as they set out to obtain the Mack truck, make a safe getaway, and fight off The Humungus's uber-violent gang, which is hot on their trail.

💡 The Inspiration

Mad Max 2 was obviously inspired by the original Mad Max film from 1979, and according to James McCausland, co-writer of Mad Max, that screenplay was inspired partly by the 1973 oil crisis's effect on Australia. McCausland noted in an article he wrote in 2006 that he was taken aback by the "ferocity" with which Australians would "defend their right to fill a tank."

🔍 REALITY FACTOR

The likelihood of a global fuel shortage is not beyond the realm of possibility. Energy crises have occurred all over the world—for example, the 2000–2001 California electricity crisis, or the 2004 Argentine energy crisis. The likelihood of a fuel shortage causing a full-scale social collapse, though, is slim. The closest it's gotten was probably the 2007 Burmese political riots that occurred in response to rising energy prices.

⚠ The Impact

✳ **Mad Max 2 was a runaway critical success.** It has a perfect 100 percent score on Rotten Tomatoes' Tomato Meter. Roger Ebert called it "a film of pure action." Richard Corliss of *TIME* magazine wrote, "Exhilarating entertainment—and a textbook for sophisticated, popular moviemaking."

✳ **Esteemed directors Guillermo Del Toro, David Fincher, and Robert Rodriguez all mention *Mad Max 2* as an important filmmaking influence.** James Cameron also cited the movie as a major influence in an interview with *The Hollywood Reporter*.

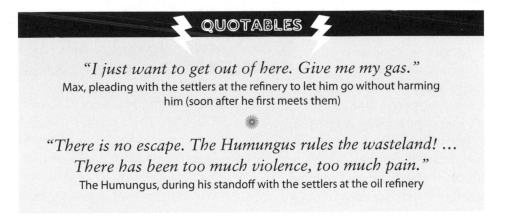

⚡ QUOTABLES ⚡

"I just want to get out of here. Give me my gas."
Max, pleading with the settlers at the refinery to let him go without harming him (soon after he first meets them)

"There is no escape. The Humungus rules the wasteland! ... There has been too much violence, too much pain."
The Humungus, during his standoff with the settlers at the oil refinery

Marisol (1992)

WRITTEN BY Jose Rivera

COUNTRY OF ORIGIN USA

Marisol, by Puerto Rican (but America-dwelling) playwright Jose Rivera, is a magical-realist apocalyptic fantasy that depicts society on the brink of a complete breakdown. In it, acid rain falls, and everyday staples like apples and coffee are extinct.

The story focuses on a twenty-six year-old Latina woman named Marisol Perez, a copywriter with a ordinary urban existence. One day, while she's riding the subway home from work, she narrowly escapes (or thinks she escapes) being attacked by a psychopath with a golf club. She's saved at the last minute by her guardian angel—a young woman in ripped jeans, a T-shirt, and sneakers. When Marisol gets home, the angel reappears and tells Marisol that although she's helped her through many tough situations, she can no longer serve as her companion. Instead, she's planning to join an angel uprising to reclaim the world from God, who's old, senile, and running everything into the ground.

The angel (Amy Stuzman) comforts Marisol (Cassie Greer) during New World Arts' 2008 performance of *Marisol* in Goshen, Indiana.

The next morning at work, Marisol's friend June tells her that a woman named Marisol Perez was beaten to death the day before (in an incident that sounds eerily like the one Marisol evaded). They look out the window and see huge plumes of smoke enveloping Manhattan. Freaked out, the

---

More Written by Jose Rivera

Family Matters (TV series, 1991)

The Motorcycle Diaries (screenplay, 2004)

Letters to Juliet (screenplay, 2010)

👁 UNFORGETTABLE MOMENT

The surreal elements of *Marisol* give us lots of unforgettable moments. One of the best is when Marisol first meets her guardian angel. The discrepancy between the angel's tough-girl exterior and her sweet, protective nature is thought-provoking. It's also just fun to imagine one's guardian angel coming over to hang out and chat for a while.

women decide to take the rest of the day off, and June suggests Marisol leave her violent neighborhood in the Bronx and that they move in together. After agreeing to the move, Marisol heads outside, only to find that the NYC she knew and loved is gone. Fires are raging and black smoke is everywhere. She's entered an unrecognizable apocalyptic landscape with no idea how she got there or what she can do to get out. Perplexed and scared, Marisol looks around for help. The rest of the play focuses on the weird string of characters Marisol meets on the street as she struggles to survive and to figure out what, exactly, the outcome of this massive angels' war will be.

ℝEALITY FACTOR

This play's apocalypse is caused by a violent war between angels and God. Cool idea, but suffice it to say, that's not an event on the calendar anytime soon.

💡 The Inspiration

Jose Rivera was allegedly inspired to write *Marisol* by the plight of his homeless uncle.

⚠ The Impact

* **The play was critically acclaimed.** Jose Rivera won the 1993 Obie Award for Outstanding Play for *Marisol*.

* ***Marisol* leaves its meaning—and even some of its plot lines—up to viewers to interpret.** The events in *Marisol* aren't totally linear, and lots of symbolism seems to be infused in the characters and the scenes. One of the biggest questions left up to the viewer is whether or not Marisol was killed by the golf-club-wielding maniac at the beginning of the play. Did she really surive, or was the whole play just a chronicle of her experience in purgatory? It's up to you to decide.

QUOTABLES

"Memorial services for Marisol Perez were held this morning in Saint Patrick's Cathedral. The estimated fifty thousand mourners included the Mayor of New York, the Bronx Borough President, the Guardian Angels, and the cast of the popular daytime soap opera As the World Turns *…"*

A homeless man nicknamed Scar Tissue, reading Marisol the *New York Post* obituary for the Marisol Perez who was killed in a golf-club attack

"Okay, I just want to go home. I just wanna live with June—want my boring nine-to-five back—my two-weeks-out-of-the-year vacation—my intellectual detachment—my ability to read about the misery of the world and not lose a moment out of my busy day. To believe you really knew what you were doing, God—please—if the sun would just come up! (To herself) *But what if the sun doesn't come up? And this is it? It's the deadline. I'm against the wall. I'm at the rim of the apocalypse."*

Marisol, first talking to God, then to herself, as she loiters on the street, unsure about what to do

Night of the Living Dead (1968)

DIRECTED BY George A. Romero

WRITTEN BY George A. Romero and John A. Russo

COUNTRY OF ORIGIN USA

Fortunately, they found a farmhouse; unfortunately, so did the zombies.

On this groundbreaking early zombie film, two siblings, Barbra (Judith O'Dea) and Johnny (Russell Streiner), are visiting their father's grave in a quiet Pennsylvania cemetery when a strange man staggers through the graveyard and begins to attack them. Barbra manages to escape, but quickly crashes her getaway car into a tree. With the zombie still after her, she abandons the car and flees into an empty farmhouse. More zombies then appear, circling the house, while Barbra tries (and fails) to call for help. Freaked out by a half-eaten corpse in the upstairs hallway, she tries to make a run for it, but someone suddenly pulls her back into the house to keep her safe. His name is Ben (Duane Jones), and he quickly goes to work boarding up the house. Barbra gets hysterical and then faints from shock.

The two soon learn that there are more people hiding in the cellar: Harry (Karl Hardman) and Helen Cooper (Marilyn Eastman), their sick daughter, Karen (who's actually been zombified), and a young couple named Tom (Keith Wayne) and Judy (Judith Ridley). Ben and Harry immediately start fighting about whether it's safer in the main house or

More Movies Directed by George A. Romero
Dawn of the Dead (1978)
Creepshow (1982)
Day of the Dead (1985)
Land of the Dead (2005)

☺ UNFORGETTABLE MOMENT

After Ben makes it safely back to the farmhouse, the camera shows what's going on outside: Zombies are eating Tom and Judy's remains, in extremely graphic detail.

the cellar. Then the group finds a TV in the house and learns that the zombie uprising is happening all over the country and that the ghouls, who are dead people come back to life, are eating whomever they kill. There are apparently fortified rescue stations in town, so Ben, Judy, and Tom risk leaving the house in a truck—hoping to get enough gas from a nearby fuel pump to drive everyone to the shelter. That plan fails when Tom accidentally sets fire to the truck, which explodes and kills both him and Judy. Zombies are afraid of fire (it can kill them) so Ben uses a flaming stick to ward them off as he runs back to the house, where Harry refuses to let him in. He busts down the door and the rest of the movie focuses on the group's futile attempts to survive. Only Ben avoids being killed

⦾EALITY FACTOR

Zilch. It's an appealingly dark and macabre thought, but dead people are, well, dead — they have not yet been known (certain spiritual beliefs aside) to ever come back to life.

and eaten by zombies, but even then the movie's message turns bleak: Ben gets shot and killed by the sheriff's rescue squad when they mistake him for a ghoul.

💡 The Inspiration

Director/co-writer George Romero first wrote a short story about zombies that he later said he had "ripped off" from Richard Matheson's novel *I Am Legend* (page 77), and that short story later became this movie. In an interview, Romero once said that he couldn't use vampires because Matheson did, so instead he used zombies—dead people who stopped staying dead.

⚠ The Impact

✳ *Night of the Living Dead*'s **pop-culture influence is massive.** It essentially created our current conception of the zombie as a staggering, flesh-hungry member of the undead. It was not the first zombie movie (1932's *White Zombie* is widely considered to take that honor), but the film's influence can be felt in scores of later zombie films, including *Evil Dead*, *Waxwork*, *28 Days Later* (page 11), and the "rom-zom-com" homage *Shaun of the Dead* (page 122). It also seems to have inspired Michael Jackson's groundbreaking music video for "Thriller," in which a posse of the undead dances to a choreographed routine.

✳ **The film became a prime example of a low-budget, sleeper hit.** Though it was produced on a paltry budget of around $100,000, it went on to gross $40 million at the box office. It also birthed Romero's

"Dead" series: *Dawn of the Dead, Day of the Dead, Land of the Dead, Diary of the Dead,* and *Survival of the Dead.*

✳ **The film was unique for having cast an AfricanAmerican actor (thirty-one-year-old Duane Jones) in a heroic lead role.** There were very few leading roles for black actors at the time. In fact, the role of Ben was originally meant to be an uneducated and crude trucker type, but after Jones's audition, Romero felt that his strength and sophistication made him the best fit the part.

QUOTABLES

"If you have a gun, shoot 'em in the head. That's a sure way to kill 'em. If you don't, get yourself a club or a torch. Beat 'em or burn 'em. They go up pretty easy."
The sheriff, advising people in a television interview on how to kill zombies

"I ought to drag you out there and feed you to those things!"
Ben says this to Harry after Harry had locked him outside amid the ghouls

Oryx and Crake (2003)

WRITTEN BY Margaret Atwood

COUNTRY OF ORIGIN Canada

Oryx and Crake, the first book in Atwood's MaddAddam book trilogy, is a novel about a future world devastated by a terrible man-made virus. Civilization has collapsed and the world has been ravaged by social inequality, large-scale genetic engineering, and human greed. The main character, Jimmy, believes he is the last human alive. The virus was engineered by his evil-genius best friend, an arrogant geneticist named Crake. The virus seems to have destroyed the population, and Jimmy's lonely existence consists of sleeping in trees to avoid being attacked by genetically engineered hybrid animals like wolvogs (wolf-dogs) and pigoons (pig-baboons), and scavenging for food. He also spends some time with the Crakers, a small community of multi-hued, genetically engineered humans specially designed by Crake to be docile and physically beautiful. The Crakers live on grass and leaves, and they recycle (i.e., eat) their own excrement. But they are dependent on humans for actual knowledge, so they now rely on Jimmy for guidance.

Jimmy and Crake had spent their teen years playing online games like Extinctathon, and visiting disturbing porn and "live execution" websites. On one particularly awful porn site, they encountered a girl named Oryx, whom Jimmy fell in love with instantly. Years later—after Crake had developed the Crakers but before he released the deadly virus—Jimmy found out that Crake had tracked down Oryx (who had been a child sex slave when they saw her online), hired her to be a teacher for the Crakers at his compound, and started a relationship with her. The book goes back and forth between the present-day apocalyptic society and the orignial love triangle, and ends with Crake slitting Oryx's throat before being shot and killed by the horrified Jimmy.

The Inspiration

While doing some birdwatching with friends, author Margaret Atwood noticed a bird called the red-necked crake. It was then that the idea for *Oryx and Crake* came to Atwood, as she wrote in an essay titled

More Books Written by Margaret Atwood
The Handmaid's Tale (1986)
Cat's Eye (1988)
The Blind Assassin (2000)

👁 UNFORGETTABLE MOMENT

After Jimmy confronts Crake inside an airtight room at the biotech compound about why he deceitfully unleashed the pandemic that's now wiping out the world, Crake slits Oryx's throat as Jimmy looks on. The horrified Jimmy shoots Crake dead moments later, and is left to grieve—and wait out the virus's destruction—inside the compound.

"Perfect Storms: Writing Oryx and Crake." She was thrown off course by the events of September 11 (in the same essay, she notes how disturbing it is to write about a fictional catastrophe when a real one is happening around you), but got through it.

⊘ REALITY FACTOR

In *Oryx and Crake*, the virus that ends up killing everyone was designed by Crake to wipe out the human race. In this act of bioterrorism, he hid the virulent agent in a new medicine he was ostensibly developing, called BlyssPlus—a multifaceted pill that claimed to protect people from STDs, provide unlimited libido, and prolong youth. Sound too good to be true? It was.

But is it possible, in real life, to hide a virulent agent in a different type of host? Yes, it is—that's often how bioterrorists do their thing. A bioterrorism attack is the deliberate release of viruses, bacteria, toxins, or other harmful agents used to cause illness or death. (See *The 12 Monkeys* Reality Factor on page 9 for more information about bioterror.)

⚠ The Impact

* **Before the book's publication, it was predicted to be a high-selling dystopian classic.** It did go on to sell well, and became a national bestseller.

* **The book was a critical success.** It was short-listed for the Man Booker Prize in 2003.

* **Atwood went on to release a sequel in 2009, *The Year of the Flood*.** That book mainly concerns a different set of characters, but it does explore the relationships of Crake with Oryx and Jimmy with his highschool girlfriend, Ren. As of 2011, Atwood was still working on the third book in the MaddAddam trilogy.

* **In 2007, Atwood said that she'd like *Oryx and Crake* to be adapted into a musical.** Her earlier work *The Handmaid's Tale* has already been turned into an opera. It has yet to happen for *Oryx and Crake*.

QUOTABLES

"When any civilization is dust and ashes ... art is all that's left over. Images, words, music. Imaginative structures. Meaning—human meaning, that is—is defined by them. You have to admit that."

Jimmy, having a mini-argument with Crake about humankind's purpose, over lunch when they're in their twenties

❋

"They noticed the remains of Crake lying on the ground, but as they had never seen Crake when alive, they believed Snowman when he told them this was a thing of no importance— only a sort of husk, only a sort of pod."

The narrator, talking about the moment when the Crakers first see their creator's (Crake's) dead body

❋

"Site after site, channel after channel went dead. A couple of the news anchors, news jocks to the end, set the cameras to film their own deaths—the screams, the dissolving skins, the ruptured eye-balls and all. How theatrical, thought Jimmy. Nothing some people wouldn't do to get on TV. 'You cynical shit,' he told himself. Then he started to weep."

The narrator, describing Jimmy's mental state as he watches, from inside Crake's compound, the world begin to fall apart around him from.

The Road

(2006)

WRITTEN BY Cormac McCarthy

COUNTRY OF ORIGIN USA

Life is not a beach for the man (Viggo Mortensen) and his son (Kodi Smit-McPhee) in the film version of *The Road.*

Cormac McCarthy's harrowing book *The Road* (made into a movie in 2009) is about a man and his son as they wander the earth after an unnamed catastrophe has devastated the environment and destroyed society. The two central characters, referred to simply as "the man" and "the boy," navigate through the charred remains of a blackened landscape without sun or seasons—an endlessly gray world where there is almost no food, animals, or other humanity. With a shopping cart full of tattered belongings and a gun with only two bullets left (to be used for protection or for suicide if they should get captured), the pair walks south toward the sea, driven by a vague notion that there will be something better there.

The journey to the coast is dangerous. The food supply has dried up to the point that people have become cannibals who capture and imprison other humans, eating them piece by piece. Pregnant women are even held in captivity so that their babies can be

More Books Written by Cormac McCarthy

Blood Meridian: Or the Evening Redness in the West (1985)

All the Pretty Horses (1992)

No Country for Old Men (2005)

👁 UNFORGETTABLE MOMENT

When the father and son stumble across a hungry old man walking alone, the boy wants to offer the old man food. But his father has only suspicion and contempt for the old guy and refuses to help him. This is when it dawns on the boy that making sure the pair act in a moral way has become his responsibility. He pressures his father to give the old man a can of fruit, and the fellow joins them for dinner that night.

a food source. The father tries to teach the son to be decent amid the horrors of their surroundings. But the father becomes ill with a hacking cough and knows he will soon be gone, so his compassion for other innocent stragglers deteriorates as he becomes more concerned about teaching his son to protect himself. The son, however, is determined to remain one of the "good guys" (a concept his father has been trying to instill in him), and in their last weeks together, the boy must now teach his father what it means to be good. The father does eventually die on the beach, and the boy finds a seemingly kind family of vagabonds to take him in.

Ⓡ EALITY FACTOR

McCarthy purposefully doesn't name the cause of the destruction in the book. Most likely, the Earth was destroyed by either a nuclear war or an NEO collision (Near Earth Object, such as a comet or asteroid). These would explain the ash and fire, toxic air and water, and the extinction of all plants and animals. Such an event *could* depress temperatures around the world, leading to a major loss of food crops and a possible collapse of society, but an awful lot of factors would have to be in place for this to happen.

💡 The Inspiration

McCarthy has said that he got inspiration for *The Road* during a visit to El Paso, Texas, with his young son. There he imagined "fires on the hill" and what the city might look like in the future, if society ended.

⚠ The Impact

* *The Road* was the recipient of countless accolades. It was selected for Oprah Winfrey's famed book club in 2007, was named the best book written within the past twenty-five years by *Entertainment Weekly* in 2008, was a finalist for the 2006 National Book Critics Circle Award for fiction, and won the 2007 Pulitzer Prize for fiction literature.

* The book was made into an equally successful film. The movie, directed by John Hillcoat, was a faithful adaptation of the book. It was admired by both McCarthy's fans and film critics for its thoughtfulness and subtlety. It also made more than $27 million worldwide at the box office.

QUOTABLES

"You wanted to know what the bad guys looked like. Now you know. It may happen again. My job is to take care of you. I was appointed to do that by God. I will kill anyone who touches you."
The man, explaining his actions to his son, immediately after shooting and killing an attacker who threatened the boy at knifepoint

"There is no God and we are his prophets."
An old straggler named Ely says this to the man, speaking about the possibility of being the last men on Earth

The Scarlet Plague

(1912)

WRITTEN BY Jack London

COUNTRY OF ORIGIN USA

The Scarlet Plague is a novella, or short novel, that's set in the year 2073, sixty years after a devastating plague has wiped out most of humanity. At the start of the story, John Howard Smith and his grandson Edwin are foraging in the woods of San Francisco (which now has less than forty inhabitants) in nothing but their animal skins. They stop to eat supper on a beach with a group of boys, and Smith begins telling his life story to the group. He first describes the plague that decimated the world's population: Infected people would develop a scarlet rash, suffer convulsions, and then succumb to a sleep-like condition before going numb, dying, and rapidly decomposing—all within an hour.

Smith had been a professor at the University of California in San Francisco when the pandemic took hold, and, at twenty-seven, he was the lone survivor among all of his colleagues. He describes the frightening way that civil society broke down after the

Jack London, author of *The Scarlet Plague*, will not stop staring at you.

plague took hold, and how the poor rose up and began murdering the rich, whom they felt had been keeping them down for too long. Smith then went off by himself to live in the Grand Canyon for a few years before

More Books Written by Jack London

The Call of the Wild (novel, 1903)

White Fang (novel, 1906)

John Barleycorn: Alcoholic Memoirs (memoir, 1913)

👁 UNFORGETTABLE MOMENT

The grandfather is telling his grandson and a group of boys about his first direct encounter with the red death. He watched a student get the plague and die within minutes in his classroom. He then headed across campus to discuss the crisis with the faculty president, President Hoag. The campus was eerily deserted except for a few stragglers here and there. As he walked into Hoag's office, Hoag bolted into an interior office and locked the door in utter fear of being exposed to the disease. That's when the grandfather realized that his life would never be the same.

coming across a few more survivors and meeting a woman to partner up and have kids with. Within a short period of time, he and the few other people left in the world were reduced to a nomadic existence.

The boys don't totally believe the grandfather's tale, and they also keep stopping him, in barely decipherable English, to ask him what various words mean. It's clear that they have no education or skills aside from

🔍 REALITY FACTOR

Mass disease has swept the world multiple times throughout history. In fact, the flu pandemic of 1918-1919 wiped out between twenty and fifty million people worldwide shortly after London's novel was published. So the idea of a disease like the one in *The Scarlet Plague* is realistic. It would have to be pretty bad, though, to wipe out the entire planet.

hunting and surviving. It also seems that even though the grandfather survived the plague, he wasn't able to pass down much intelligence, knowledge, or even the concept of compassion to the next generation.

💡 The Inspiration

Like many of London's works, *The Scarlet Plague* was inspired by socialism, a political and economic system that encourages government regulation of resources to keep everyone's wealth equal. London was a revolutionary socialist, and an adamant advocate of workers' rights. That theme can be seen in *The Scarlet Plague* when the working class bands together to kill the upper class and claim what they feel is rightly theirs.

⚠️ The Impact

※ **Though the book is one of London's lesser-known works, it was later considered groundbreaking.** Other "last man on Earth" stories had romanticized post-apocalyptic worlds and focused on their beauty or innocence, but London set a new trend by exploring how humans can devolve instead of evolve, and how barbarism can take over in a time of crisis.

※ **The Scarlet Plague influenced many later apocalyptic works.** Some of the books that seem to have been shaped by London's 1912 work include *The Moon Maid* (1926) by Edgar Rice Burroughs, William Golding's *Lord of the Flies* (1954), Walter M. Miller Jr.'s *A Canticle for Leibowitz* (1959; page 32), and Russell Hoban's *Riddley Walker* (1980). The book was also loosely adapted into an episode of a CBS radio drama called *Escape* in 1954.

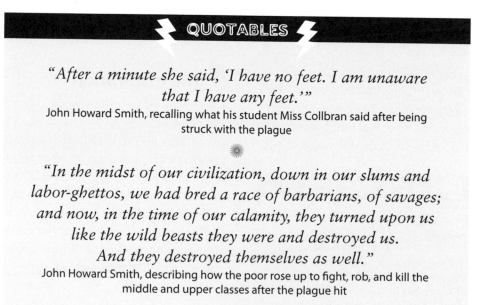

⚡ QUOTABLES ⚡

"After a minute she said, 'I have no feet. I am unaware that I have any feet.'"

John Howard Smith, recalling what his student Miss Collbran said after being struck with the plague

"In the midst of our civilization, down in our slums and labor-ghettos, we had bred a race of barbarians, of savages; and now, in the time of our calamity, they turned upon us like the wild beasts they were and destroyed us. And they destroyed themselves as well."

John Howard Smith, describing how the poor rose up to fight, rob, and kill the middle and upper classes after the plague hit

The Seventh Sign

(1988)

DIRECTED BY Carl Schultz
WRITTEN BY Clifford Green and Ellen Green
COUNTRY OF ORIGIN USA

In this scary but also kind of hokey movie set in 1988, bizarre things are happening all over the world. All the fish in the sea off Haiti have washed up dead; a village in Israel's Negev desert has frozen and shrunken to miniature proportions; and the water in a Nicaragua river has turned to blood. Two men, a Roman Catholic priest and an eerie wanderer, are both following these events and believe they signal the end-times as described in the New Testament. (The end-times are supposed to be a period of suffering that precedes the Second Coming of the Christian savior, Jesus Christ.)

The priest eventually determines that it's not actually the apocalypse. Meanwhile, the creepy wanderer makes his way to a couple's house in Los Angeles, where a very pregnant woman named Abby (Demi Moore) and her busy lawyer husband, Russell (Michael Biehn), are preparing for the birth of their first child. They'd lost one baby

Abby Quinn (Demi Moore) begins seeing horrible things (including the wallpaper) in advance of a possible apocalypse in *The Seventh Sign.*

More Movies Directed by Carl Schultz

Careful, He Might Hear You (1983)

To Walk with Lions (1999)

👁 UNFORGETTABLE MOMENT

Beginning to grow suspicious about just who exactly her renter, David Bannon, might be, Abby goes into Bannon's room to do a little snooping. She pokes around in his desk, admires his antique chest of drawers, and discovers some ancient-looking Hebrew texts sealed up with an old-school wax seal. As she leaves, she accidentally steps on the texts, and breaks the seal. As she walks down the stairs heading back to her house, the Earth begins to shake violently and the sky grows dark.

to miscarriage in the past, so they're extra careful about following their doctor's every order. The couple is renting out the room above the garage, and the wanderer, who introduces himself as David Bannon (Jürgen Prochnow), takes it. Bannon also informs Abby that he originally came to Earth as a lamb, but that now he is a lion.

Soon Abby begins having nightmares and developing some very strange fears about her pregnancy. As she gleans more information from the man living above her garage, she begins to uncover what's going on:

ⓡEALITY FACTOR

The apocalypse in the movie is pretty directly concerned with the apocalypse as it's portrayed in the Book of Revelation. So whether or not you believe the movie is possible is entirely based on whether or not you believe in the Bible's New Testament.

Bannon, she thinks, is Jesus, come to Earth to nudge things along according to God's plan—in which a baby will be born both dead and soulless, and act as the Earth's last human. While Abby is giving birth, the doctor says they've lost the baby's heartbeat. Just after this happens, Abby sees a vision of a man asking, "Will you die for him?," and she answers, "Yes, I will." Abby dies soon after this conversation, but the baby is granted life—presumably by Jesus. Abby has thus averted the end of days by sacrificing her life for her baby's, who is born with a soul like a normal human being.

💡 The Inspiration

The inspiration for *The Seventh Sign* is the New Testament's final chapter, the Book of Revelation. Written by John the Apostle in 95 AD, Revelation describes the impending apocalypse or end-times. The protagonist in this chapter is known as the "lamb" (like

Bannon) and represents Jesus Christ. In the Book of Revelation, there is a holy scroll with seven seals, which no one is able to open except Jesus. Revelation also says that Jesus will break the seven seals when he returns to Earth, thus unleashing the seven disastrous signs of the apocalypse (all of which are represented in the film) and triggering the end-times.

⚠ The Impact

⁕ **Though the movie was panned by critics, it garnered a small cult following.** People still regularly rent and buy the movie.

⁕ **It's a classic thriller relic of the 1980s.** The movie became known as a perfect example of a cheesy '80s film. It's one of those campy, over-the-top fright-fests that you laugh hysterically at while you hide your eyes under the blanket. It may not have won any Oscars, but for apocalyptic horror junkies, it's a keeper.

⚡ QUOTABLES ⚡

"Oh, God, I could feel it coming—death."
What Abby says to her husband after waking up from a nightmare about her baby

"It's called The Guf...They say whenever a baby is born, this is where its soul comes from. As the soul descends from heaven, only the sparrows can see it. So they sing."
David Bannon, explaining to Abby and Russell, over the dinner table, the spiritual concept of The Guf, a part of heaven where souls are supposedly held as they await the birth of the child they are intended to go into

movie Shaun of the Dead (2004)

DIRECTED BY Edgar Wright

WRITTEN BY Simon Pegg and Edgar Wright

COUNTRY OF ORIGIN UK

Zombies — or just an especially enthusiastic crowd of Miley Cyrus fans? Shaun in *Shaun of the Dead* doesn't care to find out.

Shaun of the Dead is a British "rom-zom-com"—a mix between a romance, zombie, and comedy movie. It opens with Shaun (Simon Pegg), a bored, twenty-nine-year-old electronics salesman, having an epically bad day. His coworkers show him zero respect and his girlfriend, Liz (Kate Ashfield), dumps him after he forgets to make a restaurant reservation for their anniversary. Dejected, Shaun heads to his favorite pub to meet his equally apathetic best friend, Ed (Nick Frost), who consoles him by telling him: "It's not the end of the world."

As the guys later stumble home drunk, they see a couple making out near the pub entrance. What they fail to notice—due to being wasted and also generally oblivious—

is that one of the lovebirds is literally eating the other one's neck. The next morning, they have an encounter with a young female zombie in the backyard, but they don't realize London is under a full-fledged zombie siege until they see TV news reports about the uprising. (They seem to be the last to know—probably because they have been living a lot like clueless zombies themselves.) Soon, more

More Movies Directed by Edgar Wright
Hot Fuzz (2007)
Scott Pilgrim vs. the World (2010)

zombies show up at their door, hungry for blood. Shaun decides they should camp out at the pub and they stop to pick up Shaun's mother, his stepfather Philip (who's been bitten by a zombie), Liz, and two other friends. The remainder of the movie focuses on Shaun's attempts to lead a battle against the zombies from inside the bar, and to win back Liz. He succeeds on both counts, but his mom, stepfather, and Ed aren't so lucky. Fortunately, although Ed is turned into a zombie, Shaun keeps him tied to the shed so they can continue to hang out and play video games.

®EALITY FACTOR

Despite what legions of horror nerds and zombie-philes would like to believe, a zombie apocalypse is not at all likely for our species or our planet. But it *is* fun to think about.

💡 The Inspiration

Shaun of the Dead was most likely inspired by an episode of the British sitcom *Spaced* titled "Art," which was written by Simon Pegg and directed by Edgar Wright. In that episode, a guy named Tim (Pegg) hallucinates that he's fighting off a zombie invasion. In reality, he's under the influence of drugs and just playing the PlayStation video game *Resident Evil 2*. The film also borrows heavily from other TV shows and movies, making for little inside jokes to the audience. The title rhymes with the famous zombie thriller film *Dawn of the Dead*; two characters from the British version of *The Office* run into each other in the movie; and when Ed tells Shaun's mom, "We're coming to get you, Barbra," it's a replay of the line, "They're coming to get you, Barbra," from *Night of the Living Dead*.

⚠ The Impact

✳ **It was a transatlantic hit.** After earning £1,603,410 (that's about $2,600,000) in the United Kingdom on its April 2004 opening weekend, the movie came to the United States. At its first screening, at the San Diego Comic-Con on July 2004, two hundred people were turned away from the door because it was too full. Another screening was added but that one also quickly filled up.

✳ **It became a cult classic.** The film won over different audiences with its unique combo of classically British witty one-liners, physical humor (parodying the horror genre), excellent slasher-style gore, and likable slacker protagonists that are easy to relate to. In the words of the movie's tagline, "In a time of crisis a hero must rise … from his sofa."

✳ **It created a new genre of film.** Everyone knows what a romcom is (romantic comedy), but no one had ever done a rom-zom-com before.

⚡ QUOTABLES ⚡

"Come and get it! It's a running buffet! All you can eat!"

Shaun says this to the zombies about himself, trying to lure the zombies away from the pub, where the rest of his friends are

✳

"We may have to kill my step-dad."

Shaun says this to Ed when he finds out his stepfather was bitten by a zombie

TV The Stand

(1994)

DIRECTED BY Mick Garris
WRITTEN BY Stephen King
COUNTRY OF ORIGIN USA

This Stephen King–penned miniseries is widely considered one of the best adaptations of a King novel. In the four-part, 336-minute series, a secret US government bio-weapons project has gone awry, releasing a deadly super-contagious flu dubbed Captain Trips. The virus devastates the United States, killing more than 99 percent of the population. The show starts out by showing us the rapid illness and death of the first man to spread the disease, Charlie Campion (Ray McKinnon), a soldier stationed in the desert who tries to flee with his wife and baby, but only serves to unleash the virus upon the population at large.

As most of the world's population (and, hence, almost everyone we've been introduced to) catches the virus and dies off, the

Nick Andros (Rob Lowe) and Mother Abigail Freemantle (Ruby Dee) play a serious game of "I spy..." in *The Stand*.

few survivors begin to have disturbingly vivid dreams of either an old woman named Mother Abigail (Ruby Dee) living in a corn field, or a creepy, dark figure with red eyes. Abigail is a prophet from God, and the dark man, Randall Flagg (Jamey Sheridan), is—for all intents and purposes—the devil. These not-so-subtle figures of good and evil essentially draw their followers to them in

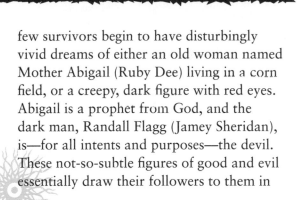

More Directed by Mick Garris
Psycho IV: The Beginning (1990)
The Shining (TV miniseries, 1997)
Masters of Horror - "Chocolate" (2005)

👁 UNFORGETTABLE MOMENT

The show opens with a chilling sequence: shots of hallways, cafeterias, labs, and control rooms full of bodies—dead within minutes from the virus. Set to the song "(Don't Fear) the Reaper" by Blue Öyster Cult, it is, quite possibly, one of the freakiest scenes ever shot for television.

their dreams, setting the stage for a final showdown in Sin City, Las Vegas.

The first two parts, "The Plague" and "The Dreams," are intense and chilling, offering an extremely detailed (and gory) picture of the panic that surrounds the first days of the virus. After the plague runs its course, the series's last two installments focus on the epic battle for the hearts and souls of humankind. This is when many think the show took a turn for the cheesy.

Ⓡ REALITY FACTOR

There are, undoubtedly, chemical and biological agents being discussed and developed in facilities around the world. But the odds of someone creating a virus that is uber-contagious and capable of killing people in mere minutes is, well, not likely. As for the biblical-style battle for good and evil? Of course it will take place in Las Vegas (or maybe Atlantic City).

💡 The Inspiration

It seems like every King fan wanted to know if his beloved novel *The Stand* would ever make it to the big screen. But because of the length (1,000-plus pages) and scope of the book, it made more sense to turn it into a TV miniseries instead of a movie. The novel was also connected to one of his earlier short stories, "Night Surf," which also featured a devastating flu.

⚠ The Impact

✳ **Warner Bros. is currently adapting *The Stand* into a feature-length film.** In a February 2011 article in *Entertainment Weekly*, King didn't seem overly psyched about this, saying he didn't know anything about it until he read it on the internet.

✳ **The miniseries was award-winning.** It won two Emmys, and was nominated for four other awards in 1994. Plus, in 1995, Gary Sinise was nominated for a Screen Actors Guild award (Best Actor) for his performace in the series.

✳ **The Stand's production company, Laurel Entertainment, took a unique "stand" for gay rights.** The miniseries was originally set to film in Colorado. But after that state passed 1992's Amendment 2, voiding and prohibiting legislation protecting the rights of homosexuals, the production moved to Utah in protest. This unique move prompted other Hollywood bigwigs including Whoopi Goldberg, director Jonathan Demme, and producer Ed Saxon to jump into the fray and call for a boycott of Colorado.

QUOTABLES

"Things fall apart. The center does not hold."
Quoting William Butler Yeats, this is spoken by an army general (Ed Harris) who kills himself after a failure to contain the disease, which means most of the human population will die

✳

"I mean, we gotta get outta the city... it's not just the odds of getting shot. You have any idea what it's going to smell like in two weeks? Five million people rotting in the July sun!"
Larry Underwood (Adam Storke), an NYC musician, talking to his new lady friend, Nadine Cross (Laura San Giacomo), after most people have been killed

movie Tank Girl

(1995)

DIRECTED BY Rachel Talalay

WRITTEN BY Tedi Sarafian, Alan Martin (comic), and Jamie Hewlett (comic)

COUNTRY OF ORIGIN USA

Lori Petty has some pretty unattractive friends in *Tank Girl*.

Tank Girl is an outrageous sci-fi romp based on a British cult comic of the same name. The film is set in 2033, years after a comet has hit Earth, changing the climate and sending the world into a water shortage. The tiny amount of available water is controlled by the Water & Power (W&P) company, led by a sadistic jerk named Kesslee (Malcolm McDowell). A mysterious anti-W&P group named the Rippers is alluded to as an almost mythical force that no one can pin down.

The main character, Rebecca Buck (Lori Petty), is a ballsy, punk-rock spitfire. She lives in a house with other misfits who have illegally built their own water well in the basement. Learning of the well, a group of men from W&P come to violently shut down the house. The only house residents who survive

are Rebecca and a little girl, Sam (Stacy Linn Ramsower), but they are kidnapped and separated by W&P.

At W&P headquarters, no matter what type of torture Kesslee throws at her, Rebecca maintains her spunky eff-you attitude. Rebecca becomes friends with another inmate, a female mechanic (Naomi Watts). Rebecca and her new friend steal a W&P

More Directed by Rachel Talalay

Freddy's Dead: The Final Nightmare (1991)

Ally McBeal (TV series, 1999–2002)

Cold Case (TV series, 2003)

128

☺ UNFORGETTABLE MOMENT

One of the film's funniest moments is when the Rippers assign Tank Girl and Jet Girl with a task to complete in order to get entrée into their community. The women must sneak into a W&P factory, dress up very glamorously, and trick W&P employees into thinking they are photographers putting together a "Men of Water and Power" calendar. They pose and photograph the men around a bunch of crates, ask them to preen in scantily clad outfits, and then immediately send the pictures back to the Rippers.

tank and a jet, rename themselves Tank Girl and Jet Girl, and set off to find Sam.

Tank and Jet soon stumble across the Rippers' hideout. The laughable-looking Rippers (one of whom is played by rapper/actor Ice T) turn out to be genetically enhanced mega-soldiers infused with kangaroo DNA. The Rippers agree to help Tank and Jet save Sam and bring down W&P.

ⓡ EALITY FACTOR

As discussed elsewhere in this book (see *When Worlds Collide*, page 146, and *Deep Impact*, page 53), there is a chance that the Earth could eventually be hit by a comet or an asteroid. But what about a drastic water crisis like the one in *Tank Girl*? There is a water shortage in certain parts of the world today. The UN has said that corruption, restricted political rights, and limited civil liberties are all part of the planet's water crisis. Overpopulation may also contribute to water crises in some parts of the world.

Together they kill a large number of W&P personnel, and Tank Girl confronts Kesslee, who has put Sam in The Pipe—a tube that traps a victim inside. Kesslee slowly fills the tube with water in an attempt to torture Sam before drowning her, but in the end Tank Girl manages to kill Kesslee, rescue Sam, and save the day.

💡 The Inspiration

Tank Girl was based on a popular British comic book created by Jamie Hewlett and Alan Martin. The punk-infused comic is different from the movie in that the comic is set in post-apocalyptic Australia (where Tank Girl lives inside her tank) and focuses more on Tank Girl's escapades with her boyfriend, Booga (a mutant kangaroo). With an extra helping of sex and drugs, it became a big hit in the indie underground comic scene.

⚠ The Impact

* **The film had a cult following, but was a box-office bust.** Famed reviewer Roger Ebert did praise the film's "enormous energy" and big ambition, though.

* **The movie's soundtrack was a who's who of '90s female rock.** The awesome soundtrack was overseen by rock goddess Courtney Love, and was full of strong women musicians including Love's own band, Hole, Björk ("Army of Me" could have been written for this movie!), L7, and Veruca Salt.

* ***Tank Girl* is one of the few apocalyptic and post-apocalyptic movies out there that was directed by a woman.** This fact only serves to enhance the film's "girls kick ass" feel.

⚡ QUOTABLES ⚡

"No celebrities. No cable TV. No water!"
Rebecca's opening narration in the film's first few moments

"Failure to recycle body fluids is a violation."
One of the rules posted on the wall inside the creepy W&P compound

"My my. She'll be fun to break."
W&P leader Kesslee, talking to himself during one of his many testy exchanges with Rebecca

V for Vendetta

(1982–1989)

WRITTEN BY Alan Moore
ILLUSTRATED BY David Lloyd
COUNTRY OF ORIGIN England

Halloween can't come soon enough for Hugo Weaving in *V for Vendetta*.

V *for Vendetta* is a graphic novel depicting post-apocalyptic England nine years after a nuclear World War III has decimated most of the world. A fascist regime has taken over and cameras on every street corner now monitor the population's every move. One man, who was imprisoned during the war and forced to be part of a medical experiment, has become an anarchist revolutionary. His plan: to kill his former captors and take down the new government. He wears a Guy Fawkes mask (see Inspiration) and takes on the secret identity of "V," naming himself after the room in which the medical experiments took place (room 5, or Roman numeral V).

One night, V saves a young woman, Evey Hammond, from being assaulted by police officers before he detonates a bomb that blows up the now-empty House of Parliament. Later, he takes Evey to live with him in the Shadow Gallery, an underground lair where he has preserved art, books, and other pre-apocalyptic treasures. At first, Evey assists V on his violent missions, but soon she questions if he is going too far. He tells her to leave, which she does, but she then ends up in prison for having assisted him. Evey realizes, while in

More Comics Written by Alan Moore
Watchmen (page 140; 1986–1987)
From Hell (1989–1998)

More Comics Drawn by David Lloyd
Hulk (1979–1980)

👁 UNFORGETTABLE MOMENT

In prison, Evey is given an ultimatum: sign a statement saying that she was brainwashed and tortured by V (to assist him in his crimes), or be shot. When she chooses death, her captors, surprisingly, set her free. She returns to V, who welcomes her home. She soon learns that her imprisonment and torture were actually set up by V as a test of her loyalty—and a way for her to experience the misery he, himself, endured.

prison, the importance of political freedom and, when she is set free (see Unforgettable Moment), she returns to V to continue the fight. When V soon dies at the hands of the police, Evey assumes this secret identity and continues with his plan.

💡 The Inspiration

V for Vendetta first debuted in a British comic anthology, *Warrior*, in 1982. *Warrior* went under before the *Vendetta* series was

ⓡ REALITY FACTOR

A nuclear war is a possibility in society, and fascists could potentially take over if we had one. (WWII was driven by fascist regimes, like the Nazis.) One of the main points in *V* is that fascist dictatorships come to power when people don't pay attention. So, in theory, a fascist society could be prevented if we all pay attention to what's going on and make sure our government (post-apocalyptic or no) doesn't get too much power.

completed, but a few years later DC Comics finished printing the rest of the series. *Vendetta*'s entire ten-issue run was later turned into the complete graphic novel.

The inspiration for the character V was Guy Fawkes. It is believed that Fawkes, along with a group of other men, conspired to blow up British parliament on November 5, 1605, as a way of rebelling against King James I for persecuting Roman Catholics. The men managed to get thirty-six barrels of gunpowder into a cellar at the House of Lords, where the king and other members of parliament were scheduled to appear that day. The plot was exposed in an anonymous letter before it could be executed. Fawkes later became an English symbol of anarchy and rebellion and his effigy is still burned every November 5 in Britain.

⚠ The Impact

✳ **The comic book was adapted into a successful 2006 movie.** The film, which was directed by James McTeigue and written by screenwriting talents the Wachowski brothers (*The Matrix*), was praised by some critics, but some felt that it deviated too much from the original comic.

✳ **The Guy Fawkes mask from *V* became famous.** The mask came to represent the idea of challenging government and authority, and has been adopted by various activist groups and worn at protests against the Church of Scientology (by the infamous internet group Anonymous), President Obama (by students at Arizona State University), the Spanish government (by protesters against a new anti-copyright legislation), and the Egyptian government (by Bostonians in Harvard Square). It's also become a popular Halloween costume.

⚡ QUOTABLES ⚡

"Strength through purity, purity through faith."
A slogan that the fascist government has posted all over the city in an attempt to convince people to have faith in the establishment

✳

"There's no flesh or blood within this cloak to kill. There's only an idea. Ideas are bulletproof."
V says this to the police before they kill him, indicating that while they can kill his body, they cannot kill the concept of freedom that he stands for

WALL-E (2008)

DIRECTED BY Andrew Stanton

WRITTEN BY Andrew Stanton, Pete Docter, and Jim Reardon

COUNTRY OF ORIGIN USA

On the distant future an overabundance of trash (most of it created by former mega-corporation Buy N Large) has forced humankind to flee Earth on a space station called the *Axiom*. The *Axiom* left seven hundred years before the movie opens, and all that remains of human civilization now is garbage, billboards, and barren establishments branded with the Buy N Large logo. (Even though Buy N Large no longer exists, there's no one left to take these things down.) WALL-E (Waste Allocation Load Lifter Earth-Class) is a trash-compacting robot left alone to clean up the planet and ready it for mankind's return. He has been doing his job for more than seven hundred years, but the task is still incomplete. In the time that WALL-E has been alone on Earth, he has become curiously human. With his cockroach sidekick — the only living creature left on Earth — WALL-E works from morning 'til night, day in and day out, building skyscrapers out of trash. At night, he escapes from the windstorms that sweep

WALL-E looks up at the stars and thinks about what he's going to do tomorrow.

More Films Written by Andrew Stanton

A Bug's Life (1998)

Monsters, Inc. (2001)

Finding Nemo (2003)

over the planet and retires to watch song and-dance numbers from the 1969 musical *Hello, Dolly!*

When a female robot probe, EVE (Extraterrestrial Vegetation Evaluator), arrives from the *Axiom* to search for evidence that Earth can sustain life again, WALL-E falls in love. In trying to impress her, he gives EVE all the evidence she needs in the form of a plant he found growing inside an old refrigerator. Soon, the two are off, back to the *Axiom* to initiate Operation Recolonize. Meanwhile on the *Axiom*, humankind has become completely sedentary and retains no knowledge of their old planet. Technically, the ship is run by Captain B. McCrea, but most of the actual command functions are handled by an autopilot robot named Auto. EVE returns to the ship with the budding plant in order to start the operation to bring humans back to Earth. But before that can begin, it falls upon McCrea to break his people out of their lazy existence in order to lead them home. In the end, WALL-E and EVE, and the humans and robots of the *Axiom*, return to Earth to fix its environment.

💡 The Inspiration

The idea for *WALL-E* first came about when Director Andrew Stanton and other Pixar creatives were brainstorming over lunch in

🔍 REALITY FACTOR

In 2009, the average American produced approximately 4.34 pounds of waste per day. Though recycling does help to reduce this amount, our recycling rate was only about 34 percent in 2009, and that number doesn't reflect the resources that also need to be used in the actual process of recycling. So while our landfills won't be exiling us to outer space anytime soon, we might keep in mind that if humankind does not keep its seemingly insatiable desire to consume in check, we really might be preparing to leave our planet to the cockroaches.

1994. Stanton didn't have an environmental or political cause in mind when he created *WALL-E*—he simply wanted to tell a love story about a lonely, abandoned robot.

⚠ The Impact

✳ **WALL-E was a smash hit among both kids and adults.** It won the 2009 Academy Award for Best Animated Feature Film.

✳ **The movie caused a stir with conservatives.** Some noted conservative pundits including *National Review* writer Greg Pollowitz and talk radio show host Glenn Beck criticized *WALL-E* for being too preachy and too liberal in its messages.

✳ **WALL-E was adapted into a popular video game.** The game was developed and released by THQ for various American game platforms in 2008.

⚡ QUOTABLES ⚡

"A is for Axiom, *your home sweet home. B is for Buy N Large, your very best friend."*

A computerized voice on the *Axiom* teaching a roomful of small children

"I don't want to survive, I want to live!"

The *Axiom*'s Captain says this to Auto, the autopilot robot, when Auto tells him that they must remain on the ship to survive

radio *The War of the Worlds* (1938)

DIRECTED AND NARRATED BY Orson Welles

WRITTEN BY Howard Koch and Anne Froelick Taylor (adaptation), and H.G. Wells (original novel)

COUNTRY OF ORIGIN USA

Lots of people doing lots of different things for Orson Welles's Mercury Theatre of the Air troupe.

In the 1930s there was an ongoing drama series called *The Mercury Theatre on the Air*, which put on live radio dramas and theatrical readings. For the Halloween episode on October 30, 1938, young author and director Orson Welles, then twenty-three, narrated an adaptation of H.G. Wells's popular 1898 novel about alien invasion, *The War of the Worlds*.

The radio show appeared at first to be a live broadcast of a musical orchestra performing in New York City's Hotel Park Plaza, but within a couple of minutes, a fictional "news reporter" (Frank Readick) broke in with information about a disturbance on planet Mars. The radio station soon returned to the orchestra, but news updates continued to break into the music saying first that a meteor had crashed into a farm in Grovers Mill, New Jersey, and then that the object that had crashed was actually an alien space-ship. People were heard screaming in the background.

Soon a number of alien hatchlings reportedly emerged from the object, and the live reporter described the appearance of repulsive-sounding creatures before the transmission stopped suddenly. Next another reporter broke in, saying that more than forty people were now dead at the Grovers

More Directed By Orson Welles

Citizen Kane (film, 1941)

The Trial (film, 1962)

Don Quixote (film, 1992)

137

👁 UNFORGETTABLE MOMENT

A news reporter says that the Martians have released a poisonous gas that is drifting over New York City and killing everyone. As the smoke draws closer to him, he says that it's "a hundred yards away" and then "fifty feet." Then he goes silent. Finally a radio operator is heard calling, "2X2L calling CQ. Isn't there anyone on the air? Isn't there anyone on the air? Isn't there anyone?"

Mill site. Soon, the Secretary of the Interior (portrayed by actor Kenny Delmar in a voice that sounded like then-President Franklin D. Roosevelt's), came on to advise the nation to stay calm despite the seriousness of the situation.

💡 The Inspiration

H.G. Wells's novel *The War of the Worlds* is the obvious inspiration for the broadcast. Wells's original novel described an alien invasion in England in the beginning of the twentieth century. Orson Welles adapted it for his radio show, placing it in New Jersey and in modern times.

ⓡ REALITY FACTOR

It is possible that life exists beyond Earth. After all, there are estimated to be hundreds of billions of galaxies in the universe. But the chances of an alien species having the super-advanced technology needed to even get here—and then to invade our planet and take it over—is relatively low.

⚠ The Impact

✳ **The show was done so realistically that people thought the world was really coming to an end.** Even though it was announced before, during, and after the show that it was a fictional program, terrified listeners (who didn't hear those announcements) deluged radio headquarters, newspaper offices, and police stations with calls for information about how to evacuate their cities and shield themselves from gas raids. Some people even required medical treatment for shock and hysteria. Orson Welles had to apologize to the public the following day, though he maintained that the show was never intended to cause a scare. When the program later aired in 1944 in Chile, and in 1949 in Ecuador, mass panic was unintentionally incited *again*.

✳ **The panic was later studied as an example of mass hysteria.** In 1940, Princeton University psychologist Hadley Cantril used the radio broadcast listeners' reactions to try and determine what had caused the panic, incorporating his findings into a book about the broadcast and its resulting chaos, called *The Invasion From Mars*.

✳ ***The War of the Worlds* inspired large-scale future hoaxes.** In 1977, the British TV program *Alternative 3* was aired in the United Kingdom. The fictional show was designed to look real, and it fooled many viewers. It pretended to be an investigation into secret government attempts to make the Moon and Mars habitable; "scientists" claimed the Earth's surface wouldn't be able to support life for much longer. Another more recent hoax happened in 1996, when, on April Fool's Day, Internet giant AOL published a fictional news flash that announced there were signs of life on Jupiter. Not surprisingly, a number of AOL's five million subscribers freaked out when they learned they'd been duped. And tech giant Google has a long history of pulling April Fool's Day pranks to confuse and disorient users. In 2004, for instance, the company posted fictitious job opportunities for a research center on the moon.

⚡ QUOTABLES ⚡

"Ladies and gentlemen, this is the most terrifying thing I have—I've ever witnessed. Wait a minute! Something's crawling out of the hollow top. Someone or something. I can see peering out of that black hole two luminous disks. Are they eyes? It might be a face.

The "reporter," describing what he sees at the scene of the alien invasion

Watchmen
(1986–1987)

WRITTEN BY Alan Moore
ART BY Dave Gibbons
COLORED BY John Higgins
COUNTRY OF ORIGIN USA

This twelve-issue comic series proposed a grim, alternate-reality version of the 1980s. In this world, society has no morals, superheroes are flawed individuals who can't save the world *or* themselves, and the Cold War never ended (see *Endgame* on page 65 for more info on the Cold War). Violence, nihilism, and black humor define *Watchmen*. A doomsday clock even appeared on the front cover of Issue I. It was initially set at twelve to midnight, but with each new issue the minute hand crept forward as the prognosis for Earth got worse.

The series' main character is Rorschach, a sullen, retired superhero who stumbles upon a plot to murder and discredit other ex-superheros. He gathers his former colleagues Dan (Nite Owl), Laurie (Silk Spectre), Dr. Jon (Dr. Manhattan), and Adrian (Ozymandias) to warn them. Soon, Dr. Manhattan, a hero with radioactive powers and a complete

Dan Dreiberg sits beside his Nite Owl uniform and wonders why he ever thought an owl would be cool in the first place. (Hoot.)

lack of human emotions, is accused of causing cancer in the government scientists he's worked with over the years. He heads off to Mars to consider his future on Earth, while his girlfriend, Laurie, teams up with Dan to resume their costumed vigilante activities.

More Comic Books Written by Alan Moore

V for Vendetta (see page 131; 1982–1989)

The League of Extraordinary Gentlemen (1999–2005)

After uncovering Adrian's evil plot, Dan and Rorschach are joined by Laurie and Dr. Manhattan in the villain's Antarctic stronghold. Adrian shows them all film coverage of the disaster, in which millions have died and all that's left of Manhattan is a smoking crater. But the footage also reveals that his plan has worked: the world has abandoned Cold War hostilities and embarked upon a new era of love and cooperation. Everyone agrees that it's in the Earth's best interest to keep Adrian's involvement a secret—the alien "enemy" is just too important as a peacekeeping device. Rorschach disagrees and rushes out to tell the world; Dr. Manhattan, motivated by a newfound love of humanity, kills him on the spot to protect the secret. Little does he know that Rorschach kept a journal of clues, which he'd mailed to a tabloid just before setting out for Antarctica.

The pair also helps Rorschach investigate his conspiracy theory, as assassins continue to strike against the group of fallen heroes.

Dan and Rorschach chase their leads right into Adrian's Antarctic lair. As it turns out, this former hero has been behind the attacks all along. He lets them in on his plan to fake a devastating alien invasion on New York City in order to give the world a common enemy and a common tragedy. When the two revived heroes kick into gear to stop the horrible plot, Adrian lets them in on a little secret: he's already pushed the doomsday button and New York is a burning ruin.

Ⓡ EALITY FACTOR

The comic features two different ways the world could end—but neither of them are particularly plausible. One is that Dr. Manhattan, a blue, radioactive giant who has real superpowers and can control things with his mind, could wake up on the wrong side of the bed one morning and decide to obliterate the universe. The second is that a violent alien invasion could take out huge portions of civilization. Neither of these scenarios should be keeping you up at night.

💡 The Inspiration

Author Alan Moore originally wanted to take over an existing group of superheroes and shock readers by pulling back the curtain on their sad personal lives. He reimagined superheroes as costumed vigilantes, and wanted to examine what kind of egotistical nut would take on such a role. Unable to convince his bosses at DC Comics to let him deconstruct any of their characters, he chose instead to create his own universe of fallen heroes.

⚠ The Impact

✷ It started a huge new trend in comics. *Watchmen* began publication the same year as Frank Miller's *Batman: The Dark Knight Returns*; together these were the first examples of comics written for adults, featuring darker story lines, deeply flawed heroes, and a generally depressing outlook on life and society. Today, Moore has said he's unhappy with the flood of "grim" and "often pretentious" imitators the series has spawned.

✷ After years of false starts, *Watchmen* was turned into a Hollywood movie in 2009. Despite director Zack Snyder's best efforts, Moore rejected the film, saying that he would be "spitting venom all over it." Moore is well-known for dissing all the films that have stemmed from his comics, including *V for Vendetta, From Hell, Constantine,* and *The League of Extraordinary Gentlemen.* Why? Because he simply loathes Hollywood, and feels it relies too heavily on the comic-book industry for ideas. Maybe he had a point in this case. The adaptation received mixed reviews and didn't do very well at the box office either.

⚡ QUOTABLES ⚡

"Now the whole world stands on the brink, staring down into bloody hell, all those liberals and intellectuals and smooth-talkers ... and all of a sudden, nobody can think of anything to say."
A snippet from Rorschach's journal, at the start of the first book

✷

"He's crazier than a snake's armpit and wanted on two counts of murder one."
A cop, describing Rorschach to a fellow officer as they investigate a man's falling death near the start of the first book

Waterworld

(1995)

DIRECTED BY Kevin Reynolds
WRITTEN BY Peter Rader and David Twohy
COUNTRY OF ORIGIN USA

The Mariner (Kevin Costner) and Helen (Jeanne Tripplehorn) rethink their earlier decision not to buy a jetski in *Waterworld*.

Waterworld is set in the future. The polar ice caps have melted, flooding the world with water. Survivors of this event are forced to continuously sail around in ramshackle boats, drink their own pee, and trade trash and debris with each other in strange makeshift societies. Mostly they are trying to avoid the gangs of evil gun-toting pirates, called Smokers, who harass people from jet-skis and airplanes (we know they're the bad guys because they smoke and drink—the mark of a true criminal!).

Kevin Costner plays the Mariner, a loner with a bad attitude. He is large and in charge, and has a seashell dangling from his ear. He also sells dirt, which is a major commodity in this world without land.

During one of his routine trade stops, some people he meets discover that the Mariner has functional gills and webbed feet (useful mutations, under the circumstances). When his deformities are discovered aboard an atoll, he is taken prisoner and sentenced to death in a pool of yellow muck. At the last minute, he is saved by the atoll's shopkeeper, a woman named

More Films Directed by Kevin Reynolds

Robin Hood: Prince of Thieves (1991)

The Count of Monte Cristo (2002)

Tristan & Isolde (2006)

👁 UNFORGETTABLE MOMENT

Near the start of the movie, when the Mariner meets up with a group of people in the hope of trading dirt, one of the men notices he has gills behind his ears. The man immediately screams, "Mutation!" and everyone within earshot begins echoing him with cries of "He's a mutant!" Then they capture the Mariner and put him (and his webbed feet and gills) in a cage, intending to drown him in sludge.

Helen (Jeanne Tripplehorn). Helen is also the caretaker of a young girl, Enola (Tina Majorino), who has a mysterious tattoo of a map on her back, which will supposedly lead whoever follows it to the world's last remaining piece of dry land.

In exchange for saving his life, the Mariner grudgingly agrees to take the two females aboard his boat. And so the adventure begins: The three search for dry land while being relentlessly pursued by the heavily armed Smokers, who are after the map on Enola's back. The Smokers eventually kidnap Enola, prompting a chase by the Mariner and Helen. When the three are reunited, they manage to find the island with dry land, and Helen and Enola stay there while the Mariner builds a new boat and sets off again to explore the seas—it's the only home he truly feels comfortable in.

Reminiscent of *Mad Max*, the movie is goofy and has some genuinely funny parts, although it's not clear how intentional they are.

💡 The Inspiration

Many critics and viewers have noted the film's striking similarity to *Mad Max 2: The Road Warrior* (see page 101), but if that were a direct inspiration, it's never been specifically cited. The director's precise inspiration is unclear.

🔍 REALITY FACTOR

Waterworld isn't too realistic. While most scientists agree that the Artic ice caps are melting, it's not happening overnight. If they did somehow melt all at once, as the movie implies, the oceans would only rise a few hundred feet—hardly enough to flood all of civilization and turn it into a floating nightmare.

⚠️ The Impact

* *Waterworld* was, for a long time, the most expensive movie ever produced, costing almost $232 million to make. *Avatar* stole the most-expensive-film crown in 2009, though, with its budget of more than $250 million.

* Despite all the money put into making it, *Waterworld* was a notorious box-office bomb. Even though it debuted at #1, it only grossed approximately $88 million— a pretty paltry figure when you consider its massive budget.

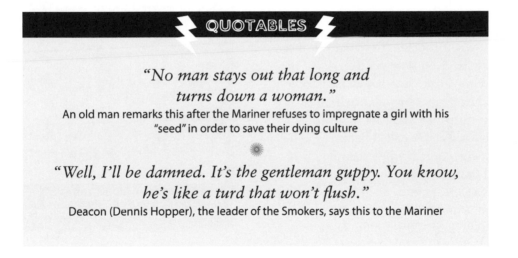

⚡ QUOTABLES ⚡

"No man stays out that long and turns down a woman."
An old man remarks this after the Mariner refuses to impregnate a girl with his "seed" in order to save their dying culture

"Well, I'll be damned. It's the gentleman guppy. You know, he's like a turd that won't flush."
Deacon (Dennis Hopper), the leader of the Smokers, says this to the Mariner

When Worlds Collide (1951)

DIRECTED BY Rudolph Maté

WRITTEN BY Edwin Balmer, Sydney Boehm, and Philip Wylie

COUNTRY OF ORIGIN USA

Pilot David Randall (Richard Derr) has been hired to transport a black box containing a set of top-secret photos from renowned South African astronomer Dr. Emery Bronson (Hayden Rorke) to the eminent New York City–based astronomer Dr. Cole Hendron (Larry Keating). The photos, it turns out, indicate that Bronson has discovered a star called Bellus, which is on a collision course with Earth. Bellus is expected to hit and destroy the world in just eight months. A planet called Zyra—currently in orbit around Bellus—is also expected to pass close by Earth around the same time.

Hendron believes that the only faint hope for the survival of the human species is to build a rocket ship big enough for forty people to escape to Zyra—which he believes is habitable for humans. Hendron alerts the US government and the United Nations about the upcoming apocalypse, but they scoff at him. Thus, Hendron is forced to obtain funding

Poster art promotes the influential 1951 film *When Worlds Collide* (in Technicolor!).

More Directed by Rudolph Maté
The Adventures of Marco Polo (1938)
The Violent Men (1955)
The Deep Six (1958)

👁️ UNFORGETTABLE MOMENT

Hendron's daughter, Joyce, also a scientist, is the first to meet Randall when he arrives. They ride in an NYC cab to bring the photos to Hendron, and Joyce talks about what is inside the box, thinking that Randall knows. Randall plays it cool, and when she asks him if he's afraid about the impending apocalypse, he shrugs it off like it's no big deal. But his shell-shocked expression tells a different story.

from less-than-ideal sources, including a selfish wheelchair-bound financier named Sydney Stanton (John Hoyt), who offers millions of dollars in exchange for a guaranteed spot on the spaceship. Soon, however, the US government takes notice of the impending disaster, and all of the people in the United States's coastal cities are forced to move inland. Hendron's rocket ship is loaded with food, medicine, equipment,

REALITY FACTOR

Scientists have repeatedly acknowledged the possibility of an asteroid colliding with Earth. In fact, some physicists believe that the destruction of the dinosaurs sixty-five million years ago may have been caused by cosmic radiation that resulted from the collision of twin stars inside the Milky Way galaxy. Could it happen again? Sure. We don't know when exactly, but we may get a close call in the not-too-distant future: Some NASA astronomers are claiming that on Friday, April 13, 2029, Asteroid 2004 MN4 will pass very close to Earth … but won't hit it.

and animals. The ship's forty passengers are supposed to be selected randomly by lottery, but Hendron reserves seats for a handful of relatives, friends, and coworkers. Scores of lottery losers, when faced with their ugly fate, use guns in a desperate attempt to strong-arm their way onto the ship. Hendron makes the brave choice to stay behind, and he prevents Stanton from boarding as well. The film closes with the ship crash-landing on Zyra (it runs out of fuel), and all the passengers disembarking onto their new home planet.

💡 The Inspiration

The film was based on the 1933 science fiction novel of the same name, which was co-written by Philip Wylie and Edwin Balmer. It was first published as a six-part monthly serial (September 1932–February 1933) in *Blue Book* magazine, where it was illustrated by Joseph Franké.

⚠ The Impact

※ **When Worlds Collide set a new visual standard for the depiction of disasters onscreen.** It was produced by visual-effects pioneer George Pal, and the effects shots were in Technicolor, making them vivid and striking. Pal also created shots of the aftermath (waves flooding NYC streets, etc.) by using small, innovative models. Though the imagery may look lo-fi now when compared to, say, *2012* (page 17) or *The Day After Tomorrow* (page 47), Pal's work was innovative at the time.

※ **The film was critically acclaimed.** It won an Oscar for Best Special Effects at the 1952 Academy Awards and was also nominated (but didn't win) for Best Cinematography.

※ **It set the stage for blockbuster *Deep Impact*.** Co-producer of *Deep Impact* (page 53) Richard Zanuck has admitted that *Deep Impact* was directly inspired by *When Worlds Collide*. You can easily see parallels in the set-up (a comet on a collision course with Earth) and the lottery, in which people are competing for a spot underground (in *Deep Impact*) or on the spaceship (in *When Worlds Collide*).

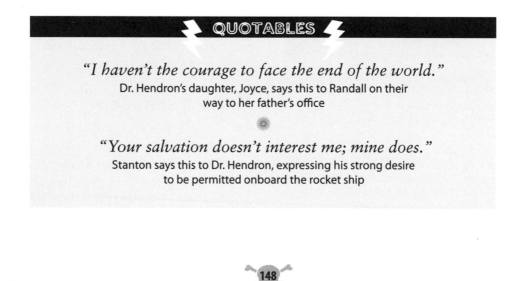

⚡ QUOTABLES ⚡

"I haven't the courage to face the end of the world."
Dr. Hendron's daughter, Joyce, says this to Randall on their
way to her father's office

"Your salvation doesn't interest me; mine does."
Stanton says this to Dr. Hendron, expressing his strong desire
to be permitted onboard the rocket ship

World War Z: An Oral History of the Zombie War (2006)

WRITTEN BY Max Brooks

COUNTRY OF ORIGIN USA

World War Z is a fictional compilation of first-person accounts, interviews, and reports about a zombie war that began after a fast-spreading worldwide plague that turned dead people into violent killer ghouls. These interviews and reports are interspersed with commentary from the book's narrator, an agent from the United Nations Postwar Commission named Max Brooks, who is collecting these bits of history to help preserve the testimony of the war's survivors.

The story begins in China, in the near future, when a zombie bites a twelve-year-old boy, who then becomes known as Patient Zero. The plague intensifies in China and then spreads to other countries via refugees and the black-market organ trade. In Africa, the disease is first believed to be rabies, and a big medical corporation, trying to cash in on the scare, develops a useless but high-selling

World War Z offers the uncomfortable possibility that zombie books could soon make the transition to nonfiction shelves.

More Books Written by Max Brooks

The Zombie Survival Guide: Complete Protection from the Living Dead (2003)

The Zombie Survival Guide: Recorded Attacks (2009)

G.I. Joe: Hearts & Minds, A G.I. Joe Graphic Novel (2010)

👁 UNFORGETTABLE MOMENT

At the beginning of the book, we first encounter Patient Zero: a twelve-year-old Chinese boy who has been tied up and restrained with packing twine behind a locked door in an abandoned house. He has rubbed off the skin around his bonds, but strangely enough, there is no blood there or on any of the other numerous wounds on his body. His skin is grey, and he has nor pulse or heartbeat. The boy is jerking violently, trying to free himself, and while doing this, his left arm snaps and bones jut through his flesh. Eventually his whole arm is "ripped completely free."

vaccine to fight the virus. Many nations don't understand the scope of the outbreak, and Israel is the only country that quarantines itself and tries to prep for a large-scale catastrophe. Soon enough, though, the world is forced to acknowledge the gravity (and grotesqueness) of the disease, and enters a stage that is later remembered as the Great Panic. The disease spreads like crazy, and it's not long before zombies outnumber humans in Africa and China. In the end, the decimation of the global population causes a change in the structure of the world: Cuba becomes the world's leading economy and Tibet becomes the most populated country.

ℝEALITY FACTOR

Um, a zombie uprising is probably never going to happen. It's fun to think about, though.

💡 The Inspiration

Author Max Brooks stated in an interview that *World War Z* was directly inspired by *The Good War*, an oral history of World War II by Studs Terkel. He also found inspiration in the classic zombie-film fare of legendary director George A. Romero (see *Night of the Living Dead*, page 107). The book also contains a wide array of contemporary references—to people like Howard Dean, Fidel Castro, and Nelson Mandela, and even the TV show *Transformers*.

⚠ The Impact

✳*World War Z* was a huge hit. Readers loved it and the hardcover edition of the book spent four weeks on the *New York Times'* Best Sellers list.

⁕**A much-anticipated Hollywood adaptation is currently in production.** Brad Pitt, Mireille Enos, Matthew Fox, and Bryan Cranston will star in the film. Brooks sold the rights in a high-six-figure deal, and a bidding war took place, with Warner Bros. and Leonardo DiCaprio's production company Appian Way battling Paramount and Brad Pitt's production company, Plan B, to make the movie. (Plan B won out.)

⚡ QUOTABLES ⚡

"'Shock and Awe'? Perfect name, Shock and Awe! But what if the enemy can't be shocked and awed? Not just won't, but biologically can't! That's what happened that day outside New York City; that's the failure that almost lost us the whole damn war."

Todd Wainio, former US Army infantryman and veteran of the Battle of Yonkers (the war that took place between the army and a massive number of zombies, in a NYC suburb)

✻

"Two hundred million zombies. Who can even visualize that type of number, let alone combat it? … For the first time in history, we faced an enemy that was actively waging total war. They had no limits of endurance. They would never negotiate, never surrender. They would fight until the very end because, unlike us, every single one of them, every second of every day, was devoted to consuming all life on Earth."

General Travis D'Ambrosia, Supreme Allied Commander, Europe

Y: The Last Man

(2002–2008)

WRITTEN BY Brian K. Vaughan
ILLUSTRATED BY Pia Guerra
COUNTRY OF ORIGIN USA

This sixty-issue comic book series is set in the summer of 2002. A Brooklyn slacker dude named Yorick is on the phone with his girlfriend, Beth (who is visiting Australia), when—in the middle of proposing to her—nearly every creature on Earth with a Y chromosome (male humans and animals) dies from a bizarre unnamed plague. Yorick is the only human male who survives. He then sets off with his male pet Capuchin monkey, Ampersand, on a dangerous worldwide quest to reunite with his new fiancée.

After all of the men die off, the world's surviving women take over all of the males' responsibilities: social, political, and otherwise. Lower-ranking female politicians get huge, spontaneous promotions—which is a huge shock in less-developed countries where societies had been male dominated. The women must also cope with the fact that humans may be doomed to extinction if they can't find a way to procreate. On Yorick's journey, he meets Secret Agent 355, a skilled female bodyguard who also becomes Yorick's traveling companion. Yorick spends much of his time on the road disguised as a woman to prevent anyone from finding out there's a remaining living member of the male species. Agent 355 introduces Yorick to a cloning pro named Dr. Allison Mann, who wants to use Yorick to produce cloned males. But Dr. Mann's lab was recently destroyed in a fire sparked by Israeli commandos, led by a woman nicknamed Alter. Dr. Mann encourages Yorick and Agent 355 to go to her second lab in California so she can start trying to clone him. They decide to go, but road travel is very slow, because food and fuel are scarce.

During the trip west, Yorick meets and becomes romantically involved with *another* woman named Beth; he eventually marries her instead of his former fiancée (whom he does eventually track down before realizing he loves the other Beth more). He also develops feelings for Agent 355. When he finally

More Written by Brian K. Vaughan
Runaways (comic series, 2003–2008)
Ex Machina (comic series, 2004–2010)
Lost (TV series, 2004–2010)

👁 UNFORGETTABLE MOMENT

The first comic book closes with scenes of men dying all around the world. Blood drips from their eyes and spurts from their mouths as they spontaneously collapse in various scenarios, like keeling over at a desk at the Space Center in Texas and falling to the ground in the middle of refereeing a soccer game in Sao Paolo, Brazil. The strips also depict the shocked and terrified reactions of the women left standing, cradling the men's heads as they succumb to the mystery ailment.

tells her this, toward the end of the series, they decide to give a romantic relationship a try. But just as Agent 355 whispers her real name into Yorick's ear, she is shot dead by Alter, leaving Yorick devastated.

It's after this that Yorick marries Beth, and they have a daughter who becomes the president of France, and Ampersand lives to become a ripe old monkey. Dr. Mann does succeed in cloning Yorick, but the men remain few and far between—and the world continues to be dominated by women.

ℝ EALITY FACTOR

It's pretty far-fetched for an epidemic to suddenly take out only the men in society, so the reality factor is low on this one. That being said, if it did occur, it's likely that it would cause some wide-scale problems and massive social upheaval.

💡 The Inspiration

Author Brian K. Vaughan has said that his series was inspired by politics and by issues that engage the reader with the real world, and also by feminism: One of his goals was to write female characters that were stronger than those he had seen in other last man on-Earth scenarios. Some readers have speculated that the Yorick character may have been inspired by Shakespeare's play *Hamlet*. The young Hamlet famously ponders his mortality when he sees a gravedigger digging a grave that once belonged to his friend Yorick, a jester in his father's court.

⚠ The Impact

✳ **The series became a cult hit.** People all over the country became addicted to the series and DC Comics dubbed it one of the best-selling comics of the last decade. Volume 10 of *Y: The Last Man* (called "Whys and Wherefores") was nominated for a 2009 Hugo Award for Best Graphic Story and, in 2008, the whole series won the Eisner Comic Industry Award for Best Continuing Series. The film rights to *Y: The Last Man* were purchased by New Line Cinema in 2007 (but the film has still not been made).

✳ ***Y* was unique and rare in that it was a feminist comic written by a man.** Vaughan has said that he educated himself by reading as many feminist writers as he could before he started working on *Y*.

⚡ QUOTABLES ⚡

"Those girls could be paratroopers or naval commanders, but men have taught them to be content behind a typewriter or radar screen. Not me."

Alter, the leader of an Israeli commando unit and a villain in the comic, describing women who aren't as ballsy as she is

✳

"It's too late. It's like this everywhere. My husband. My partner. All over the city. All over the world, maybe. It's the men ... All of the men are dead."

A policewoman says this to a distraught woman asking her for help at the start of the first comic because her little boys are throwing up blood from the plague

Z for Zachariah

(1974)

WRITTEN BY Robert C. O'Brien
COUNTRY OF ORIGIN USA

In a welcome departure from the male protagonists of most "last man" books and movies, the young-adult novel *Z for Zachariah* is written from the perspective of sixteen-year-old Ann Burden. In her diary, Ann chronicles her life following a nuclear war that has—to all appearances—wiped out the rest of the world. Somehow the Amish valley where she and her family live is spared, and though some bodies of water are contaminated by radiation, the trees are still green and nature still thrives. Her family is killed, though, when they seek help in a neighboring town. So except for her dog, Faro, Ann is utterly alone. She lives in a cave, forages for food, and tries to adjust to the fact that she may never see another human for the rest of her life.

She's shocked when, one day, a man—wearing a full-body protective suit—wanders into the valley. Ann watches silently, hidden in the woods, as he jumps into a stream that, unbenownst to him, is full of radioactive water. He soon becomes visibly ill and retreats to his tent to sleep. When he fails to emerge later, Ann decides to help the ill man. The delirious fellow calls Ann "Edward" when he first sees her, which Ann writes off as part of his delirium.

She leads him into her family's house, where she nurses him back to health while concocting fantasies about their getting married and having children. The man tells her his name: John R. Loomis. He explains that he had been a scientist who helped to design the radiation-resistant material used to make the protective suit he showed up in. Loomis also says that he was in his underground lab when the war broke out. He eventually left his office in the suit, and began looking for survivors.

On the mend, Loomis seems fairly normal—until he starts talking in his sleep. From this information Ann deduces that Loomis had shot a man named Edward (a former coworker) over possession of the protective suit. Ann grows uneasy, and Loomis tries

More Books Written by Richard C. O'Brien
The Silver Crown (1968)
Mrs. Frisby and the Rats of NIMH (1971)

👁 UNFORGETTABLE MOMENT

One of the book's most tense and heart-wrenching scenes happens late in the story, when Ann has moved out of her family's house and is sleeping in a cave to avoid being found by Mr. Loomis. Watching as Loomis encourages Faro the dog to lead him to her hiding spot, Ann has a sudden realization—she must kill Faro to avoid being detected by Loomis. She feels, in the moment, that it's her only option, because she doesn't have the guts to shoot Loomis himself. (She chickens out at the last minute.)

to attack her in a fumbled rape attempt while she's sleeping. Realizing she has no idea who she's dealing with, Ann decides to move out of the house and live in a cave. Loomis uses Faro the dog to try to track her, and he eventually shoots her in the leg in an attempt to catch her. As a last resort, Ann decides to steal his protective suit and make a run for it, but in one last meeting with Loomis the two somehow forgive each other. Loomis gives Ann his blessing and points her in the direction of a nearby town where he had seen birds flying (and where life should probably be sustainable).

💡 The Inspiration

There's not a whole lot of information about *Z for Zachariah*'s author out there, and he died while writing the final chapter of this book. (The writing was finished by his family.) So, unfortunately, his inspiration for the book remains unclear.

🔍 REALITY FACTOR

In this book, one small region (a valley) of a wider geographic area is spared from total devastation in a nuclear attack. Is that even possible? When it comes to nuclear bombs, the damage radius increases with the power of the bomb. It's possible that Ann Burden's town in *Z for Zachariah* was far enough away from the epicenter to avoid too much damage, but if that were the case, it seems doubtful that everyone else in her town would have died while she survived.

⚠️ The Impact

✳ **_Z for Zachariah_ was something of a sleeper success.** Though it's not one of the most famous apocalyptic novels out there, it was well-respected—it won an Edgar Award for Best Juvenile Mystery Fiction Novel in 1976. (The Edgar Awards are the most prestigious awards in the mystery genre.)

✳ **The book was adapted by the BBC as part of its _Play for Today_ TV series of dramatic adaptations.** It was screened on February 28, 1984. It is also in production, as of November 2011, for a Hollywood film adaptation, produced by Steve Bannatyne.

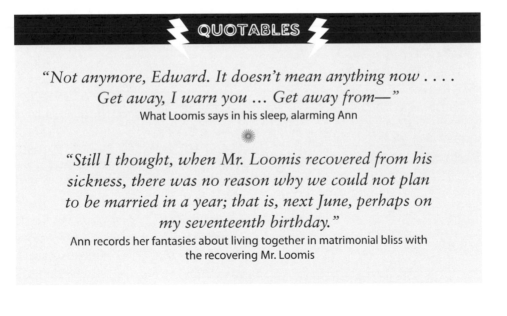

⚡ QUOTABLES ⚡

"Not anymore, Edward. It doesn't mean anything now . . . .
Get away, I warn you ... Get away from—"
What Loomis says in his sleep, alarming Ann

"Still I thought, when Mr. Loomis recovered from his sickness, there was no reason why we could not plan to be married in a year; that is, next June, perhaps on my seventeenth birthday."
Ann records her fantasies about living together in matrimonial bliss with the recovering Mr. Loomis

INDEX

ABOUT THE AUTHOR

© Tara Spalty

Laura Barcella is a freelance writer and editor who can't decide between New York and San Francisco. During the past ten-plus years, this pop-culture junkie and Washington, DC, native has written about feminism, music, news, and lifestyle topics for more than forty publications, including Salon.com, the *Village Voice*, *ELLEGirl*, *Time Out New York*, NYLON, *Bust*, CNN.com, and the *Chicago Sun-Times*.

As far as other books go, Laura is the editor of the anthology *Madonna and Me*, a book of essays by female writers about Madonna (Soft Skull Press, March 2012). She has also contributed to the anthologies *BitchFest: Ten Years of Cultural Criticism From the Pages of Bitch Magazine*, *Somebody's Child: Stories About Adoption*, and *It's All in Her Head*, a forthcoming collection about women's mental health.

When she's not writing or editing, she's reading magazines, at the movies, watching bad reality TV, eating imported gummy candy, or hanging out with animals (she has two cats and a dog, all rescues).

You can find her online at laurabarcella.com.

ACKNOWLEDGMENTS

The utmost thanks go to my parents for always encouraging and supporting my writing, both as a child and as an adult-who-doesn't-feel-like-an-adult.

Also thanks to the many friends who have listened to me talk, laugh, and obsess about this project for the past gazillion months. Special thanks to Micaella, Sarah, and Frances, who helped me immeasurably with their apocalyptic research and knowledge.

Thanks also to Karen Macklin and Dan Harmon, the editors who helped this project grow and come to fruition, and to Nikki Roddy for her fact-checking prowess.

SCHOOL LIFE

97 Things to Do Before You Finish High School
by Steven Jenkins & Erika Stalder

Been There, Survived That
Getting Through Freshman Year of High School
edited by Karen Macklin

Crap
How to Deal With Annoying Teachers, Bosses, Backstabbers,
and Other Stuff that Stinks
by Erin Elisabeth Conley, Karen Macklin, & Jake Miller

The Dictionary of High School B.S.
From Acne to Varsity, All the Funny, Lame,
and Annoying Aspects of High School Life
by Lois Beckwith

Freshman
Tales of 9th Grade Obsessions, Revelations, and Other Nonsense
by Corinne Mucha

Take Me With You
Off-to-College Advice from One Chick to Another
by Nikki Roddy

Uncool
A Girl's Guide to MisFitting In
by Erin Elisabeth Conley

POP CULTURE

Dead Strange
The Truth Behind 50 Myths That Just Won't Die
by Matt Lamy

The End
50 Apocalyptic Visions From Pop Culture
That You Should Know About...before it's too late
by Laura Barcella

How to Fight, Lie, and Cry Your Way to Popularity (and a prom date)
Lousy Life Lessons from 50 Teen Movies
by Nikki Roddy

Reel Culture
50 Classic Movies You Should Know About
(So You Can Impress Your Friends)
by Mimi O'Connor

Scandalous!
50 Shocking Events You Should Know About
(So You Can Impress Your Friends)
by Hallie Fryd

DATING + RELATIONSHIPS

Crush
A Girl's Guide to Being Crazy in Love
by Erin Elisabeth Conley

The Date Book
A Girl's Guide to Going Out With Someone New
by Erika Stalder

Dumped
A Girl's Guide to Happiness After Heartbreak
by Erin Elisabeth Conley

Girls Against Girls
Why We Are Mean to Each Other, and How We Can Change
by Bonnie Burton

Kiss
A Girl's Guide to Puckering Up
by Erin Elisabeth Conley

The Mother Daughter Cookbook
Recipes to Nourish Relationships
by Lynette Rohrer Shirk

Queer
The Ultimate LGBT Guide for Teens
by Kathy Belge & Marke Bieschke

Split In Two
Keeping It Together When Your Parents Live Apart
by Karen Buscemi

HEALTH 101

Girl in a Funk
Quick Stress Busters (and Why They Work)
by Tanya Napier & Jenn Kollmer

Sex: A Book for Teens
An Uncensored Guide to Your Body, Sex, and Safety
by Nikol Hasler

Skin
The Bare Facts
by Lori Bergamotto

STYLE

The Book of Styling
An Insider's Guide to Creating Your Own Look
by Somer Flaherty

Fashion 101
A Crash Course in Clothing
by Erika Stalder

The Look Book
50 Iconic Beauties and How to Achieve Their Signature Styles
by Erika Stalder

HOW-TO

47 Things You Can Do for the Environment
by Lexi Petronis

87 Ways to Throw a Killer Party
by Melissa Daly

Don't Sit on the Baby
The Ultimate Guide to Sane, Skilled, and Safe Babysitting
by Halley Bondy

Start It Up
The Complete Teen Business Guide to Turning Your Passions Into Pay
by Kenrya Rankin

Where's My Stuff
The Ultimate Teen Organizing Guide
by Samantha Moss with Lesley Schwartz

TRUE STORIES

Dear Teen Me
Authors Write Letters to Their Teen Selves
edited by Miranda Kenneally & E. Kristin Anderson

Regine's Book
A Teen Girl's Last Words
by Regine Stokke

Zoo Station
The Story of Christiane F.
by Christiane F.